AF650413

Reflective Practices and Professional Development in Teaching

Reflective Practices and Professional Development in Teaching

Sandeep Kumar

SHIPRA

All rights reserved. No part of this publication may be reproduced or transmitted, in any form or by any means, without prior permission of the copyright holder and publisher.

The opinions and views expressed in this book are of the author(s) own and hence should not necessarily be attributed to the institution where s/he is employed and s/he is solely responsible for plagiarism & copyright issues, if any that arises.

₹ 895
ISBN: 978-93-88691-72-7

First Published in India in 2021

Reflective Practices and Professional Development in Teaching

© Sandeep Kumar

Published by:
SHIPRA PUBLICATIONS
LG 18-19, Pankaj Central Market
I.P. Ext., Patparganj, Delhi 110092, India
Tel.: +91 11 2223 5152/6152
E-mail: info@shiprapublication.com
www.shiprapublication.com

Contents

Preface

Continuous Professional Development (CPD) has been understood in various ways. There are many theories and perspective to explain CPD, yet the question of product and process, with reference to CPD, has always been a concern. On the one hand, CPD is perceived as an outcome in the form of what one has achieved; on the other, process is considered more significant. Certain CPD methods have been considered for decades, but till date none has been fully accepted and implemented.

Today, schools are more profit-oriented and the teacher's role, consequently, is regarded as providing that benefit to the school. Thus, the school has become an open market, where the teacher's growth, development and space have reduced. In such a situation, this book will provide teachers the space to develop more professionally.

This work provides enough space to develop a comprehensive perspective about CPD, wherein without changing the situation, one can try to change the teachers' perspectives and ideas towards their profession and processional growth. One of the objectives of the book is to help teachers to make sense of what is knowledge and how children construct it. It is essential to engage teachers to understand this process of knowledge construction, as this engagement will help them to become familiar with the process of how knowledge is constructed by learners and how they perceive others' knowledge.

Different issues related to theoretical and practical aspects of CPD are included in the book. It provides a broad framework to deal with such issues within the school system. The book may help teachers to understand CPD beyond mere financial benefits, and would help them in developing a sense of commitment towards their teaching profession and using various ways and techniques for their professional development, such as, using models of reflection, the reflective journal, mentoring, peer collaboration and so on. This book should be an asset for the in-service teachers, pre-service teachers and teacher-educators, who wish to develop as reflective practitioners.

I am grateful, first and foremost, to the people who were not directly engaged in this process but allowed me to spend time for this work, i.e. my parents, wife and kids. They supported me without any complaint and demand. My sincere thanks goes to research scholars–Rohit Vaidhwan, Akhilesh and Utkarsh who helped me a lot in completing this work. I also express my special thanks to the schools, teachers, and B.Ed. students, who participated in my various conducted studies, and their continuous collaboration helped me to explore the unexplored dimensions of Continuous Professional Development and reflective practices.

Sandeep Kumar

CHAPTER 1
Introduction

There are many reasons for teachers to develop as reflective practitioners. Perhaps, the most important is that teachers need to be reflective, in order to deal with the inevitable uncertainties and trade-offs involved in everyday decisions that affect students' lives. We are living in a complex and diverse world. The way our society is diverse, our classrooms are also diverse and this diversity ranges from visible to invisible spheres of social and personal life. Caste, class, gender, disabilities, other kinds of special need of learners, make the teaching profession more challenging. Teachers are also governed by certain conceptions, ideas and ideological positions, which make their work more crucial and difficult. The variation in thinking and believing patterns (diverse thinking in learners and teachers' own thinking patterns) generate almost invisible base for prevailed practices in schools. Given all the complexities, ambiguities, and dilemmas that characterise today's classrooms, effective teachers will need to engage in both, critical inquiry and thoughtful reflection, for their continuous professional development (CPD). No doubt, this can never happen with tailor-made changes in existing system. Need is to critically analyse the system internally by the people engaging in everyday practices in such systems. In school setting, teachers have to take this responsibility and for this they have to be given space and opportunities to develop their idea of practice with regard to broad view of CPD instead narrowed view where everything is given just to be implemented. The prevailed ideas and practices about continuous professional development is not facilitating in achieving the objective to make teachers reflective practitioners. Teaching is a complex and dilemma-ridden endeavour, necessitating ongoing learning, as well as the capacity to be reflective. Therefore, it is important to see the development of reflective practice, as the foundation for the highest professional competence.

But how many school and university teachers actually consider reflective practices important is a question to be researched and explored further. It has been proved, by many researches, that students and faculties at school and university levels do not take reflection as a part of their work. Therefore, they hardly reflect upon the work and achievement they are engaged with. This ignorance creates problems and roadblocks to express one's emotions, feelings and thoughts, whereas the role of reflection is highly educational and professional. It provides opportunities to learn through experiences. Beyond this, it provides space to develop oneself professionally. It is important to mention that reflection starts from others, but reaches the individual, where individuality is not separate from the community. It is important to know that reflective practices enhance the critical ability in teachers and make them capable of dealing with all kinds of situation effectively. Reflection is a process and it develops while consistent engagement in its process. It cannot be given but can be developed. Appropriate opportunities will help teachers to become reflective. It is also important to mention that teachers also should not accept sudden change and improvement rather must have patience and consistent engagement in practice which provide critical and reflective engagement. Many such practices are mentioned in the book in further chapters.

The idea of this book was not conceived as many other books. The book is a compilation of many small and longitudinal researches conducted by the author *(Funded by University of Delhi, under the Research and Development Scheme)* which contribute directly or indirectly toward continuous professional development and reflective practices which help teachers to understand teaching profession in a broader sense. So, the idea of this work was to provide a comprehensive understanding about teaching, learning and professional development with reflective practices.

The work is unique and different in that a great deal of field experiences of the author and school teachers have been incorporated. It, thus, provides a balanced perspective of CPD, through reflection, incorporating both the theoretical, as well as practical dimension.

The second chapter presents an elaborate understanding regarding continuous professional development, along with its existing situation in schools. It also elaborates upon teaching as a profession and its codes of conduct. The first section of the chapter incorporates theoretical and practical aspects which strengthen the chapter, where the current situation is presented, on the basis of field realities. The chapter also discusses the need and importance of CPD. Further the chapter discusses teaching as a process in details along with codes of conducts in teaching profession. It incorporates Underlying Principles to Decide Code of Conduct and then detailed codes of conduct based on said principles. As we do not have fixed codes, therefore, codes of conduct discussed in this chapter are broad frameworks along with specific practices such as codes of conduct with regard to learners and parents, with regard to work expected, with regard to profession and professional community itself, and with regard to society/community. It provides a detailed and comprehensive understanding about these codes and associated practices. NCF 2005 and NCFTE 2009 have also been analysed to locate its contribution for teaching as a profession, and responsibility teachers must consider important.

Reflection is a significant process of CPD and carries a philosophy with it. These philosophical bases of reflective processes are discussed in Chapter Three. This chapter presents the different steps and levels of reflection. Three levels of reflection named Instrumental learning, Communicative learning, Emancipatory learning are discussed in detail. Reflection and reflective practices have also been discussed with reference to *Schon* and *John Dewey*. The Chapter also discusses about theories of action and learning process, where learning has been explained in two directions: Single Loop Learning and Double Loop Learning (Argyris and Schon, 1974).

Different models of reflection are discussed in Chapter Four, where four models of reflections: Gibbs', John's, Kolb's and Driscoll's are explained. Insights gained from open-ended interviews, with practising teachers, have been discussed. They were asked questions, such as what they understood from 'reflection', if and how they practised it, what, according to them, the need and importance of reflection were, and so on. The four models of reflection were discussed with the participating teachers and they were asked to comment on the merits and demerits of these models as well. Finally, a new model of reflection is proposed, based on the teachers' responses. This model incorporates a sequence of steps or stages named Experience, Reflection, Analysis (aided in students input), Changes, and Implementation. This process moves in a loop and works as unending process. Unending means, this process is ever moving and evolving. Teachers keep learning and developing new insights to become an active reflective practitioners.

Reflective processes are complex, but with conscious efforts are doable. This conscious effort needs extensive deliberated thinking and action, as practitioners face many problems. This process of conscious effort and the teachers' struggle for CPD and reflective practices is presented in Chapter Five. The Chapter makes efforts to help reader to develop a comprehensive understanding of understanding teaching professionalism. During the course of understanding teaching professionalism various challenges faced by teachers have also been discussed. With the help of various thinkers, it explains teaching profession as social construct. The chapter also discusses the role of teacher as learning specialist, counsellor, administrator and moral guardian.

Reflective practices will remain incomplete, unless the practitioner is aware about his/her own way and pattern of thinking. It is crucial to know about metacognitive process in thought process. Ways of knowing is also being explained with relation to reflective practices. Chapter Six extensively explains these processes and talks about how we construct understanding the ways of knowing. With the help of a study conducted, various ways of knowing are discussed which emerged during the conduction of the study. These ways of knowing are: Accepted Knowing, Subjective Knowing, Process Oriented Knowing, Discrete and Apart Mode, Joint Mode and finally Constructed Knowing. These are explained with essential characteristics of each.

For the teachers' professional development, it is significantly important, that they should be aware and have knowledge about various existing practices of CPD. Such awareness will develop a strong knowledge base about CPD. Teachers must be aware of the different methods of professional development and should have a strong CPD knowledge, which have been developed and presented in Chapter Seven. Various ways to promote better classroom dealing are discussed such as Analysis of Practices, Exposure to Alternatives, Decision regarding Methods etc. Along with these practices, different challenges have been highlighted, which a teacher faces during the course of becoming a reflective practitioner. Some suggestions to deal and overcome from these challenges are also discussed in the chapter.

This knowledge base requires knowledge regarding different reflective practice ways, such as reflective journal writing, diary writing and so on. A reflective journal is an effective CPD tool. Chapters Eight and Nine are devoted to journal writing and diary writing. Chapter Eight argues that every teacher thinks about various concerns, but need is to think about all such concerns in an organised manner so that a better working environment can be developed. Various perspectives on reflective practices strengthen the quality of the chapter. Chapter Nine analyses the diaries of some teachers, who agreed to become part of the work proposed by author. Their experiences clearly prove the role of journal and diary writing in their professional development. 'Why should we even keep a reflective journal?' 'How do we go about it i.e. writing a reflective journal?' 'How reflective journal enhance teachers' ability to be critical and reflective about the practices?'– are some of the pertinent questions being addressed in the chapter. Methods of reflective journals such as double-entry journals, stream of consciousness writing, mind mapping etc. have been given due space in the chapter.

Chapter Ten elaborates the teachers' research as a CPD tool. The chapter argues that Continuous Professional Development (CPD) is the need of the hour for teachers across the world. However, it is true that most professional development for school teachers is being organised by outside agencies, such as SCERT and so on, which usually conduct annual seminars and workshops for teachers during the summer break, which hardly facilitates teachers' continuous professional development, as nothing like follow-up programmes exists with regard to this, which has been substantiated by school teachers here in the chapter. Thus, an argument has been developed, in favour of a system, which is part of the the school-teacher's everyday life, facilitating their professional development. For this purpose, 'teacher research' has been seen as an effective process. A study in Delhi schools has been conducted to provide practical strength to the discussed idea of 'teacher research'. This study incorporates the teachers' experiences, learning and developed perspectives during the span of the study, as a teacher researcher. The chapter further discusses the theme that has emerged from the analysis. Teachers experiences as researcher are incorporated with regard to their understanding of CPD.

In present time a great value is being given to education. It is important to understand how successfully teachers have understood the idea of teaching and professional development. A project was taken up to understand the relation between reflection and metacognition. This includes the documentation and analysis of the process of reflective practices of various teachers. As a result, meta-cognitive model has been developed for reflection. This also provides space and knowledge about how to improve teaching. This work is a great contribution in the field of reflective practices for improving professional development of teachers, which is presented in Chapter Eleven. The Chapter also elaborates upon how varied contexts play significant role in engaging with reflective practices, therefore, there is no single way or pattern of reflection; rather, there are ways of reflective practices. Academic, social efficiency, developmental, social re-construction and generic orientation of reflection are few of such ways.

Professional development and the Learner-centered School is the title of Chapter Twelve which is again a fieldwork-based chapter. The Chapter argues that the traditional form of professional development programme will not be able to help teachers for long, for example, programmes organised by some outside agencies. In contrast, based on teachers' experiences, an outline of learners-centered school-based professional development is discussed. It argues that CPD is not only for teachers, which generally is the case and being perceived in prevailed practices. It is beyond this simple explanation and takes it to the level of a clear relationship between teacher and learner. The required objective of CPD of teachers can only be achieved when it is based on child-centric approach instead only teacher-centric. The argument of individual CPD is also being questioned in the chapter and CPD is seen as collective process for the schools. It has also been seen as social community practices. CPD has been explained with reference to the following:

- Based on learners' performance.
- Focus on systemic development of individual.
- Action research in teaching and learning.
- Job-oriented professional development.
- Content for professional development.
- Short term versus long term plans.
- Professional development is not occasional; it is embedded in everyday life.
- Professional development is the responsibility of all, not of few.

Action research and reflective teaching have a reciprocal relationship, which has been presented in Chapter Thirteen. The chapter discusses the relevance, importance and ways of reflective teaching. It perceives reflection as a process bridging different gaps that exist in the teaching learning process, the teachers' professional development with reference to teaching, learning, learners, knowledge, classroom practices and so on. The Chapter discusses reflection as a bridging process between available and not available, knowing and expanding further. This bridging has also been seen between theory and practice and also generating new ideas. Who is a reflective practitioner and how should s/he work is also elaborated in the chapter. What is important to keep in mind is that this elaboration is not absolute, rather, there are various ways because of diverse needs. The chapter also establishes the need of reflective practices for CPD.

Along with reflective teaching, mentoring is discussed in Chapter Fourteen, emphasising the need for a school-based professional development programme. Mentoring is being presented as an effective practice to provide school-based CPD for teachers. It can be understood at three levels in the chapter i.e. initial orientation, improving professional practices and developing teaching as a professional community. The beauty of the proposed mentoring scheme is that it does not work on the principle of hierarchy where one is superior to another, rather it works on mutual role reversible process, where at one time mentor works as mentee and another time mentee works as mentor. This proposed idea is based on collegial relationship. Discussion over the benefits of mentoring for teachers and students have also been discussed. At a larger level, the chapter questions the exitsting professional development practices and proposes a collaborative, reflective and progressive mentoring idea for CPD.

The last chapter discusess the benefits and challenges regarding reflective practices, as a whole. Certain possible solutions, with reference to the given challenges, are discussed. The Professional Learning Community (PLC) has been accepted and discussed as an effective practice for CPD through reflection. The benefits of reflective practices are discussed with reference to flexibility, practicality, professionalism, sustainability and so on. The Chapter provides optimistic idea to think and work upon to develop better space and opportunity for CPD of school teachers.

Each chapter has its unique importance in the CPD of teachers, through reflection. The work is beneficial for school teachers, students of different types of teacher education programmes and teacher educators, in order to develop a comprehensive perspective about reflective practices. The purpose of this book is to equip teachers to become familiar about the importance and significance of reflective practices in their professional development. The process of CPD through reflection is very slow process and needs patience but it is very effective process which makes a teacher independent to own the responsibility of his/her own professional development.

CHAPTER 2

Continuous Professional Development and Code of Conduct of Teaching Profession

The idea of Continuous Professional Development (CPD) along with existing practices and situation of CPD in our context is discussed in the chapter. Further, the chapter establishes teaching as a profession along with certain ethical code of conduct expected to be associated with teaching profession. It deals not only with code of conduct but also the fundamental principles that should work behind these codes of conduct. The development of a comprehensive perspective about the prevailed practice of CPD and role of teachers as a professional is the objective of this chapter.

What is CPD?

The strength and quality of any profession largely depends on how it manages the three stages of *preparation, induction and the on-going development* of its members. The acronym CPD stands for 'Continuous Professional Development' or 'Continuing Professional Development' and, broadly, signifies the process of continuing growth of a professional, after joining the profession. To understand this term better, we need to look at its three parts or components: continuous, professional and development. The word '*continuing*' or '*continuous*' suggests that the process of learning goes on, even after entering the profession. Consequently, the individual is not stuck nor feels stagnant in his/her professional life. Its function is to help one review, reflect and improve one's learning and performance. It aids one in identifying, further developmental needs. The word '*professional*' suggests one's dedication to one's profession, although it does include personal development. The word 'professional' emphasises responsibility of the individual and the institution. Looking at the final word of the acronym CPD, the word '*development*' suggests that the individual is constantly evolving and updating himself/herself, according to his/her professional needs and requirements.

CPD for Teachers

The pace of change in society has compelled virtually all people, educators in particular, to give due weightage to the need for lifelong learning. Continuing professional development means maintaining, improving and broadening relevant knowledge and skills, in one's subject specialisation and one's teaching and training, in order that it has a positive impact on practice and the learners' experience. The first requirement of CPD for teachers is that they are treated and respected as professionals. The willingness and capacity for lifelong learning, which we expect from our students, should also be reflected in our teachers. Every teacher should be a continuous learner in order to advance the quality of our education system and the quality of students' learning. The professional development needs of teachers vary from person to person and from school to school. CPD should, therefore, enable individual teachers to make meaningful self-evaluations of their learning needs over a wide spectrum of professional experience. It must enable schools to address the professional development of their entire staff in a manner consistent with established theory and effective practice. While the need for a new emphasis on teachers' continuing professional development has been widely acknowledged, it is less obvious how this can be realised in a meaningful, well-planned and coherent manner. Teachers have a responsibility to be professionally up-to-date and strive for continuous, personal growth and professional excellence, through lifelong learning. Also, teachers, as professionals, have a responsibility to facilitate the professional growth and development of their colleagues.

Informed teaching and professional practices improve students' learning. The all-round development of teachers is as important as the all-round development of students and schools are prominent contributors to the wider community, as they provide models and space for continuous development for teachers. Equally important is the teachers' passion for continuous learning and self-improvement. In this era of knowledge expansion, globalisation, high technology and rapid social transformation, the belief in effective learning, as an on-going process, is a fundamental tenet of professionalism in teaching. In this regard, CPD plays an important part in providing teachers with reference descriptors that assist them in identifying their own strengths and developmental needs.

Two Views of CPD

Different people understand CPD differently. In education, we can find two views on CPD: the *narrow* and the *broad views*. The *narrow view* considers CPD as the imparting or acquiring some specific set of skills or knowledge, in order to deal with some specific new requirements, such as introduction of new textbooks or inclusion of new technology for teaching. This view imposes CPD workshops on teachers and treats it as the sole responsibility of administrators and institutions, as facilitators. This also works as top down model where authorities will organise CPD workshop for teachers. The underline assumption in this top-down model is that teacher themselves cannot do their own professional development and, therefore, external agencies have to organise such programmes. This model is also known as *deficit model*, where, what a teacher can do is not the focus point rather what a teacher cannot do is focused and training is planned to learn what they are not able to do. The impact of such CPD programmes do not help teachers much as gradually teachers also become dependent on other agencies for their own CPD. Such programmes are one-time events and hardly there is any follow-up. Such practice helps system much lesser than the expectations.

The *broad view* of CPD is a much deeper and long-term process, in which professionals continuously enhance not only their knowledge skills, but also their thinking, understanding and maturity. Training is just a part of CPD, and not all of it. They grow not only as professionals, but as persons as well. CPD is a continuous and lifelong process, whereby teachers try to develop their personal and professional qualities, to improve their knowledge, skills and practices, leading to their empowerment, the improvement of their agency and the development of their organisations and their pupils. This view can also be seen as growth model of CPD, where, teachers have to play an active and constructive role than simply accepting what is given by external agencies. Teachers' ability and strengths are given more value to what they are not able to perform. It works in a continues manner and not as one-time affair. This proposed many practices, based on teachers' collaboration and sustainable in school system with minimum external intervention. Such broad view where training, filling mind with various available methods and telling what is to be done in a given situation, objective is to enhance abilities and thinking processes of teachers to help them grow and develop as reflective practitioners. These reflective practitioners will generate their own mechanism to deal with diverse kinds of situations. It is also important to know that any specific method will not help in all situations. Every situation is unique in its own way, so need is not to provide readymade solutions, rather need is to develop capacity in teachers to develop various ways to deal with diverse situations they face every day.

We may also refer to the broad view of CPD as the 360-degree view of CPD. It considers the previous experiences of the teacher and is adaptable according to specific needs. The emphasis, in this view, is on the teachers' self-initiative for their own development. For holistic development, responsibility and voluntarism are expected of teachers.

Different Methods for CPD

- Action research
- Writing reflective diaries/journals
- Peer observation and mentoring
- Writing portfolios
- Social networking with other professionals
- Maintaining a professional development log
- Participation in relevant conferences and seminars
- Gaining further qualifications
- Creating support groups
- Participating in online courses and networking.

Current Situation of CPD

The current situation of CPD, for school teachers, is subject to enquiry, as, except for some seminars in the summer vacation, nothing concrete and useful takes place. These seminars are not taken seriously by the school teachers or the organisers, as the genesis of this problem lies in the policies and their recommendations. Almost all polices associated with education have talked about in-service education and professional development. However, their recommendations have become redundant, but we are still following them. Thus, instead of facilitating the process of CPD, this hinders it.

This is not representative of the entire recommendations of all policies, but, an overall analysis regarding developing and understanding CPD would help in understanding its purpose. Some recommendations justify the need for CPD, but no concrete plan or action layout has been suggested. Other recommendations have talked about developing and creating space for CPD and different elaborative ideas have been suggested, but how such space can be made available for teachers, has been ignored. We are still stuck on an outsourced CPD model. These out of school agencies develop CPD programmes for teachers, which includes workshops or seminars and have been mostly rejected by the school teachers themselves (as will be discussed, at many places in further chapters), as they mentioned that these seminars do not help them and are a complete waste of resources and time.

Teachers are far more interested in a system, which is self-sustained in school and on-going. But, mostly, teachers do only simple teaching, administrative work and endless correction work. They mentioned that they lost enthusiasm to teach, over a period of time, as the system did not allow them to think independently. It seems that they just do lots of routine work, without engaging in reflective processes. Teachers also mentioned that pre-service programmes, such as B.Ed., B.El.Ed. etc. hardly help them to sustain in the system and, very soon, instead of changing the existing system, they become a part of it.

Some of the teachers highlighted the drawbacks of RTE for their CPD. They very explicitly mentioned that RTE and CCE has ruined the system very badly, as products of such a system will not be knowledgeable and will pass without knowledge. This situation de-motivates teachers towards their CPD. With regard to this, their involvement in non-academic work is another hindrance.

Therefore, first, there is a huge gap between what the policy says and what actually happens. Second, the policy's understanding about CPD, through workshops and seminars, is inappropriate and third, the ethos, working condition and environment do not provide space for an appropriate CPD.

This book will definitely facilitate the CPD of teachers and other reflective practitioners. The idea of the present book is to create and present a relationship between CPD and reflective practices.

Teaching as a Profession and its Code of Conduct

We understand that teaching and associated practices certainly carry ethical aspects, but we have to understand the very ideas that having ethical aspects and living with those ethical aspects in given spaces are two distinct things. It is like, theoretically we believe that we must behave honestly and should work toward social welfare but in practice it is not true in the same intensity as we believe it in theoretically. It is not true with human only but also in teaching-learning processes as well. It possesses a kind of ambiguity due to constitutively ethical nature of teaching. This inconsistency between what we know and what we do in teaching profession is not new. People like Carr (2000) and Strike (2003) have talked about this concern. A great change or we can call it shift has taken place in education where different attractive terms have been floated such as delivery, competencies, abilities, skills, training, etc. These terms and ideas challenge the basic ethical and professional nature of educational practices. Other aspects have also challenged the ethics in education, such as the way 20th century philosophy perceives and contributes educational practices; thinking and policy construction have contributed toward restlessness in the whole domain of education, if not vetoed completely, on the basis of what they expect to be essential with regard to educational practices and educational and ethical thinking. If one has to explain this vacuum space, the left out of metaphysics in the philosophical disposition of social science can be seen as one of the strong reason and switching to producing a person as per the demand of the 'social market'. This idea has made current education, specifically teaching, largely evidence-based, delivery driven, measurable, standardised and demonstrative' and on the other hand, demand to make teaching such a practice which is ethical in nature. We have reached a level of analysis where technology and technocratic solution are seen as ultimate solutions. This view has gradually started explaining education largely based on objective facts and empirically supported data which is ethically neutral.

Teaching as Profession

Understanding teaching as profession will lead us to many ambiguities and impasses where it is difficult to address raised questions from the viewpoint of professions other than teaching, because teaching is not a profession same as others, rather it has its root in social service. However, there is no doubt that teaching is also a profession and there are various aspects which establish this claim. Some of the aspect of teaching as profession are discussed below:

It Engages in Intellectual Working

Teaching is expected to engage and work towards intellectual practices with regard to teaching, learning and other associated practices. This includes a major responsibility on teacher to develop or create an encouraging and favourable environment which facilitates learning process of students. Therefore, teaching profession has to be an intellectual engagement.

No Universal Practice

Teaching as a profession does not have any universal practice which is acceptable by all. We also need to understand that teaching is neither only science nor dependent only on scientific practices. Teaching has 'sociality' as one of the fundamental characteristics. This sociality gives space for uniqueness of all learners in school and teaching-learning processes. So, we will be on mistake if we consider teaching only as a science. It does not mean that teaching does not need planning. Certainly, it requires planning, but not in terms of final output or in absolute objective sense, rather in terms of spaces where phenomenological aspect of teaching-learning are given required importance (value).

Knowledge or Information

Teaching profession has to make a clear understanding about information and knowledge. Teacher must understand whatever they share with learners, work as information for them, their interpretation of the information becomes knowledge for them, but for another person this generated knowledge will work as information. Therefore, we need to work on this principle that there is no universal knowledge rather there are multiple realities. The propaganda that there will be a final definite solution needs to be questioned and challenged.

Self-organisation is Essential Aspect

Teaching profession demands self-organisation for better development of self as a practitioner and professional. One has to develop his/her one ways and mechanisms which govern their own ways of thinking and practising ideas they are convinced with. This self-evolution provides strength to the teaching profession.

Teaching Profession as Social Service

Teaching profession is to be considered as social service where larger objective should be to make learner aware and confident about their own strengths. Serving society via school and learner should be the prime objective of teaching profession. Teachers have to be a motivator to work toward developing a better society.

Free from Interference

Teaching profession should not be intervened unnecessarily. Any interference in curriculum development, teaching practices, classroom activities, setting up objectives etc. create hurdle in teaching profession. External forced obligations (political, social, economic, etc.) always disturb the self-evolved and governed processes of education and teaching.

Systematic and Organised Body of Knowledge

Every profession has some systematic organised body of knowledge, which provides a shape and scope to the profession and associated discourse. Education and teaching profession also have a systematic and organised body of knowledge as it has knowledge based on systematic research. Teaching profession has its own epistemology which contributes in generation of new knowledge to the profession. Different spheres of human life also contribute to the teaching profession.

Common Codes of Ethical Conduct

Teaching profession has certain common codes of conduct which may or may not be written but they do exist, and teaching profession works on underlying principles of these codes of conduct. Some of these principles are discussed later in this chapter. These codes of conduct organise teaching profession in and with ethical sphere and establish teaching as profession.

Teaching as a profession is different from many others. Not only in terms of the nature of task expected but also because it does not have accepted code of ethics as other professions such as medical etc. This situation makes it essential to talk about and consolidate and propose the codes of ethics for teaching as a profession. This objective makes it essential to revisit the existing and proposed possibilities. We can understand it in two ways; *first, basic principles which work as a baseline to set the rules* and *second, the set rules themselves.* Largely the second one dominates. However, we will be discussing both underlaying proposed principles and proposed rules which collectively provide teaching an established sense as profession.

There are different documents available across the world which talk about the codes of ethics for teaching as profession. What is proposed here is based on the analysis of such available discourse. Let us first discuss about the proposed principles on which various rules will be proposed in next section of the chapter.

Underlying Principles to Decide Codes of Conduct

Preparation

It is essential for every profession to have certain basic knowledge and skills which is to be given to concern professionals so that they can contribute not only to the field concerned but to a larger society with the idea of interdisciplinary approach or perspective. This does not mean that everyone should be given same set of knowledge, but space must to given to evolve as a professional who is able to generate the ways of preparing oneself to contribute the field one is engaged with. This preparation is self-governed and organised.

Recompense (Compensation)

Recompense is very important principle for developing codes of conduct. It is accepted that social contribution of every professional is important but, on the other hand, what professionals are getting is also important. The assurance, salary, social approval, membership of professional organisations etc. are some of the examples of recompense for professionals. This recompense definitely motivates them to contribute to the field. It also helps them to understand that certain specific ethical practices are acceptable whereas others are not. This remuneration should be such that teacher should be independent to meet the living expenses. This will detain them to work other than teaching and they will contribute at their best.

Social Service

The most important aspect or principle of codes of conduct is that professional should work for social service and for social welfare. They should not be focused only for their individual development and growth, rather their focus should be on larger social welfare. Teacher should be servant of society and not the master of it. The profession of teaching should not be reduced to the mere idea of politics, religion, caste, gender etc., rather it must see people as human beings and should work towards their wellbeing. We understand that teachers are also part of the community, but they should always keep community interest prior to their personal interest.

Responsibility Towards Learners

The most important obligation of teacher is toward students. They are teachers because there are students, so the prime principle on which teachers' codes of conduct should be based upon is students. The teachers' professional activities should be organised around learners so that what is expected can be made available to learners for their better development. Teachers' activities should be fundamentally organised as per the need of the students and this is the fundamental ethical code of conduct.

Cooperativeness

Another essential principle underlying code of conduct is cooperative attitude of teachers towards all stakeholders in education such as learners, parents, colleagues, educational administrators and other officials. Teaching profession can work successfully based on this cooperation because education itself is a social enterprise and it should take place in a cooperative environment with cooperative attitude. This collaborative effort contributes in students' development in all spheres.

Professional spirit

Any professional work becomes effective when people who are engaged with it have strong and positive professional spirit. They should not do work with the compulsion that they have to do, rather they should do it with inner motivation, in other words, the locus of causality should reside inside the person. This spirit is surely and largely associated with learners' need and social service/welfare. This spirit also incorporates commitment, concern, care, humanity, rationality, honesty and many more such attributes which help a professional to disseminate his/her expected duty effectively with no external force, pressure or enforced consensus.

Based on aforesaid principles one can elicit many and various kinds of rules for codes of conduct. These rules or codes of conduct can be seen and understood with regard to many contexts such as; *with regard to learners and parents, with regard to work expected, with regard to profession and professional community itself, with regard to society/community.*

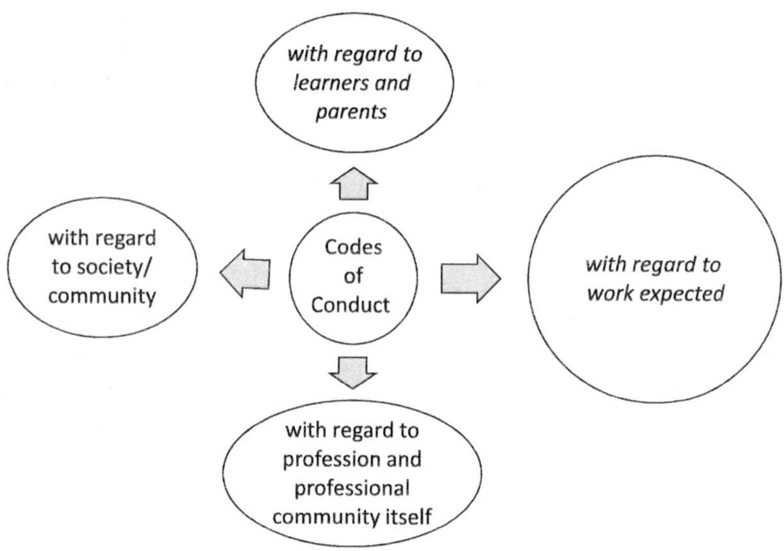

Fig. 2.1

In next section of the chapter, these 'regards' are discussed in detail.

With regard to Learners and Parents

- It is important for a teacher to understand and respect the uniqueness and individuality of students. They need to give value to each learner instead of considering them as homogenous group. Preference should be given to learners' interest with positive attitude of acceptance. Teacher must deal with all students without any kind of preconceived notion and partiality. They must be aware of learners' social and economic context but not for discriminating rather organising learning spaces as per the need of the learner.
- Respecting learners as they are, is another important value a teacher must possess. Teacher should not comment on anybody's cultural practices, moral values, physical appearance, which makes them feel inferior. This will develop a kind of confidence in learner to talk to teacher without any hesitation.
- A teacher should not accept any additional remuneration except salary. They must perform their best in class while teaching without any aspiration of getting any special monetary benefit.
- Teacher must be aware about the ways and means which cause any kind of harm and exploitation of students. They must work to save children from all such conditions. If they are failing to do this, they must bring such situation to public notice so that people can take required action as larger social group. But the larger agenda must be to save the children and providing them adequate learning environment.
- Teacher should offer additional help to those learners who need extra support in comparison to other learners. This will make classroom an inclusive space for learning.
- A bridge needs to be developed between school and family. This bridge will bring a close connect between teachers and parents and this collaboration will eventually help learners to explore best possible opportunities available. While developing this connect teacher must be working on the principle of 'non-discriminatory practice', where teacher develops a positive rapport with all parents.
- Teacher should encourage and motivate parents to take active part in providing adequate developmental opportunities to students.

With regard to Work Expected

- It is also significant for a teacher to work towards strengthening the education with the collaboration and support of all stakeholders in education whether teaching or non-teaching officials. This will help teacher to understand and know the responsibility s/he has to perform as long as school spaces are concerned. Teacher must be critical towards school system, practices and rules but for the improvement of it. In all, teacher must contribute positively with administrative system of school to make school a better social place for children.

- A teacher should obey all the rules made by authorities, but it does not mean that teacher will not be critical about situations, rights and responsibilities. A teacher must perform the role of critical friend towards education and school system.
- Different kinds of policies contribute in strengthening quality of school education. Teachers must contribute in education policy making directly or indirectly and if they are not given that space, they must demand for this collaboration to make a better school policy. They must demand democratic process of school policy making.
- Teacher should always maintain the correspondence and dialogue with school official.
- There is a mechanism of organisation which works in the base of entire school system. Teachers must respect this organisational system. It can also be understood as how school system functions. There must be some important principles, underlying those organisational practices and teacher should respect those.

With regard to Profession and Professional Community itself

- It is teacher's responsibility to set and maintain required standards of various aspects which make teacher a role model for many. Teacher must work sincerely towards standards like justice, equality and morality in such a way that they can become role model for learners. It implies that teacher is expected to perform more than teaching in a classroom. For example, teacher must present himself/herself as a person, as they want their student be like.
- Open-mindedness is an important aspect of the quality of teacher. A teacher should always be a student and should have progressive ideas about education and knowledge. This open-mindedness and progressive thought will allow him to be flexible in relation to theoretical perspective and ideas. S/he will not be rigid to one idea or perspective only. Moreover, s/he will become critical about evolving perspectives. It also implies that teacher must read about new ideas and knowledge emerging every day.

- A teacher must be a researcher. This expectation from a teacher is essential, as s/he deals with learners and is aware about the challenges and problems learners face more than any other officials. This generates the necessity of a 'researcher teacher'. Teacher not only does research, rather shares his/her research with others for larger contribution.
- Teacher must deal with his/her colleagues with collegiality which is based on mutual respect and acceptance. Though this mutuality does not mean accepting everything blindly, but becoming a critical collegial friend is the basic idea. This collegiality also includes inclusive language, caring, honesty, helping and supporting each other with positive attitude. Cohesiveness among teaching community is also expected from teachers.
- Teacher is not expected to be activist but s/he must raise voice against unethical or immoral professional practices because s/he has certain professional commitments. These professional commitments are associated with larger teaching community and expected to be performed by every individual faculty member. This will make teaching profession a worthy and socially responsible profession from various points of view.
- Teacher should not deprecate the teaching profession and should work to make it a larger social practice where positive analysis of practice is valued rather than only criticised. Teacher must work toward establishing teacher as a 'teacher', with all positive practices and attributes to oneself and education as a larger system. In other words, teacher must respect and protect the dignity of the profession and teachers.
- What a teacher does in profession is important, but a teacher must also motivate others to join the profession. This motivation will automatically enhance the value of teachers and teaching profession in society.
- The consistent commitment makes a professional effective and authentic because professional due to consistency will have lived experience which will contribute largely to the teaching profession. So, a teacher must not join teaching as a ladder to reach somewhere, rather they must join this profession with commitment and should contribute their best to it. They should nurture it to the best of their abilities.
- We all are biased toward ideas, ideologies and perspectives and so the teacher, but it is important for a teacher to present a balance and unbiased view to the learners and then let the learner develop

their understanding. So, teacher should not present one-sided idea or view rather provide spaces where learner can engage in developing their perspective.

With regard to Society/Community

- A teacher must try to meet the standards of social expectation. It does not mean whatever a community expects a teacher should do, rather it means teacher should understand the expectations of social community from a teacher and s/he should try to meet those expectations. This deals effectively with characteristics of teacher which includes willingness, internal desire and commitment to serve the social community.
- A teacher must engage with society and societal practices so that a connect/bridge can be developed between school and society. This bridge will develop automatically when teaching will be related to society. That is the reason why it is expected from a teacher to be researcher not only in school but in society as well, so that authentic bridging can be developed with authentic practices. This can gradually be conceptualised as teacher's contribution to community.
- A teacher must prioritise people's interest over his/her personal interest. This rule is linked to the social service principle mentioned above. It does not mean that teacher should not think about himself/herself at all, but larger focus must be on social welfare.
- Teacher must not use educational forums for any political agenda, rather s/he should present academic perspectives of the shared concerns. The academic rigour where learners learn to be critical, analytical and reviewer should be promoted by the teachers.
- Teacher should not take any additional benefit from people such as gifts etc. Such practices will definitely deviate them from their actual work and motivate them to take undue advantages of the position they are working on. Teacher is not a commission agent.

No doubt, teaching is not only a complex process rather it is a multi-dimensional engagement with an ever-going process of learning and constructing meanings. It has been a dominating view that teacher is the source of knowledge and therefore, students' learning is dependent on teachers. This belief has given teachers an authoritative role to play in learning. But from past many years, the prevailed ideas about learner, teacher, learning and knowledge have been revisited and reconstructed around the centrality of the learner. NCF 2005 has visualised teachers' role different from the past. It expects teachers to work as facilitator in learning process where s/he contributes as co-constructor in meaning making process. It is also important to know that only knowledge about instructional strategies will not help entire process, rather teacher has to work multifaceted such as teacher as learner, action researcher and counsellor.

Teacher is a lifelong learner. There should not be any time when teacher can claim that s/he has learnt everything. This thinking will hinder the process of actual teaching-learning process required to take place in school. Their lifelong learning will maintain if they visualise themselves as researcher. A researching teacher will always be exploring to become better and more capable in facilitating learning process of learners. Such developed abilities will definitely make a teacher capable to guide or counsel the learners in their learning process. NCFTE 2009 has also defined a constructive role of a teacher.

The detailed study of NCFTE 2009 also indicates certain codes of conduct which can be derived from the role of teacher expected in the document. Some of them can be seen as given below:

- Teacher should be a facilitator, knowledge constructor, responsible, sensitive, committed towards justice and social reconstruction.
- Teacher must understand that learner is not a mere receiver of knowledge. A child constructs knowledge himself/herself in the due course of learning via interaction and negotiation.
- Teacher must see learning as researching the meanings with analytical and reflective practices.
- Teacher must understand that it is essential to link theory with practice. So, teacher must try to make classroom learning and real life experiences a meaningful whole for learner.
- Teacher must organise learner-centered activities, where all learners can participate and share learning experiences.
- Teacher must encourage learners to critically assess the given content and do not take it as absolute. Teacher must motivate learners to raise questions.
- Teacher must develop learning activities with the help of learners. This will develop ability of independent learning in the learners.
- Teacher must engage learners in authentic experiences so that that they can understand the relevance of teaching.
- At larger level, it is teacher's responsibility to develop social sensitivity and collective consciousness to develop better sensibility in learners.

- Teacher must use hands-on experiences as effective pedagogic tool to facilitate learning and connecting learning with outside world.
- Teacher should also work towards providing training and education critically to promote peace, democratic values, justice, equality, liberty, secularism, etc.

Summing up

Teaching is a profession or not, has always been debated. This debate also rises because education has not been considered as discipline. It is because it has been argued that education largely takes its content from various other disciplines such as philosophy, psychology, sociology, etc. It is also important to note that emerging trend in education is to 'theorise from the field' which can break the monotony of looking towards other disciplines to understand educational concerns. Not only this, we are also moving towards a world where interdisciplinarity is the solution to the problems. Despite all debates and consensus, it is a fact that profession does not have any officially, legitimate and legal code of conduct, in the way other professions have such as law and medicine. Various documents like NPE, NCF 2005, NCFTE 2009, etc. have tried to lay down certain expectations from teachers but these are only expectations and an organised practice of codes of conduct for teachers is still missing in the system. It does not mean that nothing exists in this regard. Every institution definitely has some system/mechanism of working but such system faces difficulty in absence of relatively few nationally accepted codes of conduct. Nationally here does not mean to compromise with the importance and value of contextuality, rather it means that work is to be done to generate a community of practice which adheres with certain expected roles and responsibilities and stands along with other professions with maximum capability and strength to achieve the highest expected role or objective.

CHAPTER 3

Reflection Process
Practice and Philosophy

Reflective practice is an evolving concept. Therefore, it is most useful when we are able to situate it in a general framework, which can provide both, a direction for the evolution of the concept and its present dimensions. This chapter develops a framework, which would help us in understanding reflection, as a concept and its relation to learning for both students and teachers.

Teaching is firmly located within academic fields or disciplines. The latter have been broadly categorised in terms of their epistemological structure (Donald, 2002), mainly their cognitive aspects, that is 'hard versus soft and pure versus applied' (Biglan, 1973), and, sometimes, their social dimension, that is 'convergent versus divergent and urban versus rural' (Bêcher, 1989). 'Epistemological structure' continues to be a central theme in higher education teaching literature (e.g., Bêcher, 1989; Donald, 2002; Neumann, 2001); so is 'reflective practice' (e.g., Beaty, 1997; Clegg, 2000; Campbell and Norton, 2007). Nonetheless, empirical studies, investigating whether academics' reflective practice on teaching takes on distinct forms, due to differences in the epistemological structure of their chosen field, are scarce.

Relationships seem to exist between 'epistemological structure' and 'conceptions of teaching', learning, types of knowledge valued, reflections on course design, educational purpose, as well as the styles of formal inquiry into teaching and learning. There are tensions between encouraging disciplines to develop their own styles of pedagogical inquiry and observations that these 'styles' delimit the focus and scope of such work, thereby possibly curtailing some of the development opportunities inherent in the notion of 'reflective practice'. The acceptance of reflection, as a valid mode of learning, is essential in discussing and optimising the benefits of reflective practices, as only then can we acknowledge the value attributed to the notion of 'reflective practice' in teaching. This stems from the widely held view that reflection on teaching experience contributes to the development of more sophisticated conceptual structures (Leinhardt and Greeno, 1986), which, in turn, leads to enhanced teaching practice and, eventually, it is hoped, to improved student learning.

Philosophers, educationalists and psychologists have offered varied perspectives on the meaning of reflection. *Dewey's (1991, 1910)* classic definition as "judgement suspended during further inquiry" (p. 13) has been complemented by Schôn's (1983), well known distinction between reflection-action and reflection-on-action and Kolb's (1984) elaboration of the role of reflection in the transformation of experiences. King and Kitchener (1994), associate reflection with a capacity to render considered judgement in the context of ill-defined problems, and critical theorists continue to link reflection to notions of a critique of ideology and knowledge (Brookfield 1995; Freire 1971; Habermas 1971).

Given such diverse orientations, it is not surprising that efforts aimed at arriving at a generic model of reflection, continue. It is unclear how systemic reflection is different from other types of thought. Does a mere participation in the study group or keeping a journal qualify as reflection? If a teacher wants to think reflectively about or inquire into her/his practice, what does she/he do first? Can one learn reflection, or its process?

Rohit Dhankar makes an interesting point about teaching reflection to teachers, flatly rejecting the claim that one can teach someone the reflective process, but, yes, definitely, one can help teachers become reflective practitioners through this difficult yet satisfying path. He states, 'Reflection builds on what one already knows – systematically, logically, and imaginatively – to reach where one wishes to go. It is an exhaustive and difficult process; may not always be enjoyable; actually, could be quite tortuous. In fact, the greatest joy in reflection comes at the end of the tunnel, when one glimpses some faint ray of light.'

He categorically distinguished between 'reflection' as a skill (something related to practice which, generally, relates to teaching strategies), rather the understanding of, actually, what one is doing. Reflection scores a point on that aspect, questioning and reformulating the belief systems and the assumptions (thus, automatically increasing efficiency and skill set of practitioners).

The next question arises, what exactly are we looking for as evidence of reflection? Are personal enough? Are there specific criteria that can guide assessment?

According to Mezirow (1991), content (not the subject content), process and premise reflection, are qualitatively different; indeed, they represent different levels of reflection, which constitute a continuum of increasing complexity. Similarly, in their empirical study with six academics, McAlpineet al., (2004), identified three types of reflection: first, reflection that principally draws on existing knowledge, second, reflection that questions knowledge and third, reflection, which leads to a construction of new knowledge.

These three broad processes/levels of reflection are, again, linked to or integrated through three orientations of learning.

- *Instrumental learning:* Instrumental learning is essentially based on the 'scientific method'. We validate our knowledge claims by posing them as a hypothesis, which we then test (for example, "*students will respond better to my teaching, if I make certain changes to the course*"). However, a fact-driven descriptive approach to learning about teaching that does not emphasise interpretation (for example, keeping a record of students' grades, comparing end of course evaluations, and so on) are also principally of an instrumental nature
- *Communicative learning:* In communicative learning, we validate our knowledge, as we engage in dialogue within a community to achieve a shared interpretation on our assumptions (for example, we might discuss the meaningfulness and relevance of certain values that, presently, guide our curriculum planning).
- *Emancipatory learning:* Emancipatory learning involves reflection on premises, the questioning of core beliefs that define how we presently interpret our practice (Kreber and Cranton, 2000; Mezirow, 1991). We might question, for example, why particular goals, values and practices are valued within the department or community and critically examine the processes and conditions by which these have evolved. It is closely related to critical paradigm. The works of Paulo Friere, Henry Giroux and so on have a significant impact on evolving these practices. The legitimacy of questioning traditional structures and practices in creating new knowledge is fundamental. As a teacher, reflection would allow us to limit our role of perpetuator of the state and society's repressive practices.

At both micro (classroom) and macro (school as a system) levels, "emancipatory learning involves reflection on premises and presuppositions, so is there an alternative?" We question the questioning of core beliefs that define how core beliefs (on which the definition of our problems depends) presently interpret our practice.

Although instrumental, communicative and emancipatory learning are distinct, all three can be involved in the same learning activity.

Chris Argyris and Donald Schon suggested that two *theories of action* are involved in learning. These are those theories that are implicit in what we do as practitioners and "intellectual labourers", and those on which we call to speak of our actions to others. The former can be described as *theories-in-use.* The words we use to convey what we do, or what we would like others to think we do, can be called *espoused theory.* Learning can progress through two directions: *Single Loop Learning* and *Double Loop Learning* (Argyris and Schon, 1974).

Single loop learning is associated with detection and correction of errors. This process suggests opting for a new or different strategy, if one is going wrong (within the governing variables). It focuses more on operationalisation, rather than questioning.

Double loop learning provides spaces to question the governing variable for critical scrutiny. This learning can provide spaces to alter the existing governing variable and, therefore, change in strategies, as well.

Donald Schon focused on two dimensions of reflection, i.e. reflection *in action* and reflection *on action.* The former has, at times, been explained as 'thinking on our feet'. It is associated with our experiences, feelings and our theories in use. It facilitates our understanding about our action and unfolds the existing realities, in a new form.

The reflective practitioner gets him/herself ready to face surprises, conflicts or confusion in a situation, which he/she finds unusual. He/she reflects on the phenomenon before him, and on the prior understandings which have been implicit in his/her behaviour. He/she carries out an experiment, which serves to generate both a new understanding of the phenomenon and a change in the situation (Schon 1983: 68).

The concept of reflection-in-action alone misses the "social nature of practical knowledge" (Usher et al., 1997). They contend that "reflection strategies are maximized when co-learners are encouraged to make [and articulate] connections between theory and practice" (Schell & Black, 1997, p. 23).

Reflection, as a process, has been influenced and effected by many theories, related to philosophy and pedagogy. Constructivism is one such approach, which favoures that learning is an active process, where learners reflect on their past and current knowledge to construct new knowledge or understanding about a concept.

John Dewey defined reflection as a proactive, ongoing examination of beliefs and practices, their origins, and their impacts (Stanley, 1998). Reflection, as a process, has also been influenced and effected by many philosophy and pedagogy theories, Constructivism is one such approach, which favoured learning an active process, where learners reflect on their past and current knowledge to construct new knowledge or understanding about any concept. A *humanistic* element of reflective practice is its concern with personal growth and its goal of liberation from values that can limit growth (Kullman, 1998).

Critical pedagogy has been misunderstood as an approach. Actually, it examines the underlying power and strategies, emphasising active implementation, testing, and refining of ideas through experience, which shapes reflective practices.

Foundations and Characteristics of Reflective Practice

In reflective practice, especially in teaching, practitioners, usually, engage in a continuous cycle of self-observation and self-evaluation, in order to question and comprehend the basis of their own actions and the reactions they prompt in themselves and in learners (Brookfield, 1995; Thiel, 1999). The aim of the endeavour is not, necessarily, to solve any specific problem or question at the outset, as in practitioner research, but to observe and refine practice, in general, on an ongoing basis. It is, in this aspect, different from self-evaluation or self-assessment.

The following steps are integral to the reflective process:

Collection of Descriptive Data

Gathering information about what is happening in the class, to understanding the details and class perspective, is one of the important tasks of reflective practice. This can be achieved through selected data-collection tools. There are various ways which help to get a clear picture, namely, the practitioner's writings of his/her experiences, the learner's views, through their colleagues and experiences and existing theoretical perspective. Rohit Dhankar sums up the basis of the practice of reflection by stating '*'reflection' involves looking back, looping, being conscious of what one is doing; this is an activity of 'looking at oneself'; not in a narcissistic manner, but as a critical other. Kabir said that keep the critic close by, make a hut for him in your own courtyard, one has to go further to be a reflective person: has to imbibe the critic as part of one's own self; one has to become comfortable with playing two roles simultaneously – that of a practitioner and of a disinterested critical witness.*'

Thus, when we say we can use four possible ways or frames of references to collect data, it serves the sole purpose of integrating these two selves.

Analysing the Data

After data is collected, it has to be analysed, in terms of beliefs, assumptions, attitude, objectives, power relations reflection. The following questions can be asked of the data collected (Crandall, 2000; Gebhard, 1996; Stanley, 1998) and the analysis may help to understand the surprise and relationships that exist between theories of teaching and learning, which is implicit in the data; how do these theories relate to the practitioner's stated beliefs and attitudes; what are the consequences of the practitioner's actions and *considering the alternate or parallel scenario, where the situation or activity could have been different.*

Whether looking at the data, 'in the moment', or 'in retrospect', practitioners need to examine two things simultaneously: first, the choice one has made and second, the beliefs behind that choice. It is important to see how other practitioners address similar situations, generating alternatives and asking "what if" questions that push practitioners to broaden their reflection beyond the data they have collected (Gebhard,1996). It is at this stage that the writing style of a reflective journal or models of reflective style, become significant. The guiding factor remains the same: to train your thought processes on what could have been different from what actually happened. The very crux of reflection lies in this step and learning to maximise instructional efficiency. Even when we might not have better alternatives, at least, we have a record of our own self-critique, so that, perhaps, when we return to the class months or years later, we will know the areas in which we need to do more research and preparation.

Developing a New Plan to Consider New Insights

Reflection is not conducting for its own sake, rather, it has to improve the instructional practices, which can only happen if a practitioner is able to make links between the knowledge and insight gained from reflection and classroom situations, to change for positive growth. It is not important that the change is huge, as small change can have a good effect on teaching and learning (Gebhard,1996). The important thing is to incorporate insights from reflection in planning and decision-making for new action and, again, observe new action for further reflection, to maintain the process of the reflective cycle. This stage epitomises the fact that reflection and reflective practice is a continual learning exercise.

The process of reflection, with respect to the practices and its inherent nature underneath, can be viewed to consist of *three aspects or levels,* through which the reflective process actually evolves:

a) *Descriptive*

This aspect of reflection, basically, serves as a fodder for further, complex levels of reflection. It serves the purpose of 'data', a collection to base our reflective analysis. As we know, reflection is an ongoing process and learning cannot be limited to a frame of time or understanding. The critical self, which, as stated earlier in the chapter, is the aim of adopting reflection, as a regular part of our teaching style, is never static or given. The growth of our own self, in the light of our efforts to be more efficient as teachers and facilitators of learning, will result in different insights of the same experience or events. Especially for a beginner practitioner, it gives a platform or launch pad for a more complex analysis.

Statements, which help in or are based on this aspect, would somewhat look like this: write down key subjects, examples, assignments or activities used in class; describe any successes or failures that you observed and record any student comments that you want to remember.

Apart from being a handy source of data, which can serve as fodder for further analysis, it provides a quick reality check to evaluate the efficiency of our practices. A different frame of reference to look into our practices and inherent assumptions go a long way in deepening our understanding of the dimensions of our selves.

b) *Comparative*

Consider how another instructor might have taught the same class or consider how students, with different learning styles, might have responded to the instructional methods you used. This level builds on the descriptive level and, over a period of space and time, analyses one's own practices with set references or parameters. Another major benefit of reflective practice is the ability to evolve a dynamic reference (or parameter) on which a comparison can be made. A highly flexible and efficient reflective practice (built on empirical data, produced by practitioners themselves) can encompass the subjective and complex nature of the teaching and learning scenario. It can provide an intra-personal avenue for growth, allowing comparisons over one's own practices, over a period. A very ironical description is of an event where two teachers arrived for a job interview with the same qualifications and same experience of teaching for twenty years. But, when one of them was selected and the other rejected and on asking why, the recruiter responded that the selected person had twenty years of teaching experience and the other had 1 year into 20 times of teaching experience. The professional growth does not just mean counting the years of teaching, but how you have improved your practice with the context and contributed to the field. This involves experimenting and building a repertoire of knowledge and skills.

c) *Critical*

The highest order of thinking occurs in the critical dimension of reflection. There are two different ways in which reflective teaching can be 'critical'; in the sense of considering broader implications and deeper meaning of classroom instruction (Jay and Johnson, 2002), and in the sense of self-critique and continuous learning and improvement. In trying to prompt different kinds of reflective thinking by teachers in training, the practitioners can use journal writing and write 'what moral or ethical issues were raised' in their teaching experiences. The range of moral and ethical issues could start from classroom issues, to sociological factors affecting teaching or education.

Some of the critical reflection of this dimension will come, not only in the writing the journal, but, also, in reading it. Student evaluation comments might well send us back to our journals, looking to see how we might have created a certain impression or communicated an approach that we did not intend. This level evolves when one starts asking questions such as, how does one know if one is getting better at doing it? To what does one aspire?

Without a clear picture of what reflection looks like and without a common language (practitioners often use words and terms that have overlapping meaning such as, reflection, inquiry, critical thinking, metacognition), the reflection process can lose its basic agenda of 'meaning making' (Dewey,1910). We have to be very careful not to slide towards this side.

"Reflective thinking is an ongoing process and should continue after the student's teaching experience." The following can be optimally explored: using a teaching journal, peer collaboration with like-minded professionals, dimensions of reflection as a framework for considering various learning events. The most optimal usage of the two ingredients of successful professional growth is 'interaction' and 'continuity' that define where the reflection process should be focused.

Teachers, especially beginner student teachers, should develop their own notion of what teaching is and have a reasonable command over the practice of teaching, otherwise they will have no basis for any organised experience to reflect upon.

They should develop the habit of being as fully aware as possible of their practice and its impact on children and be critical of it. This is a disposition which can only develop, if one is committed to the teaching profession and cares for children.

Reflective practice requires a commitment to continuous self-development and the time required to achieve it. Practitioners should be trained in reflective practice and given time to experiment with and master the general process. Reflective practice may prove to be emotionally challenging, but, if sustained, gives unparalleled satisfaction and self-worth to teachers. Some practitioners may not be ready to confront the uncertainty about their teaching philosophies and competence that can be a part of the process. Therefore, to counter the emotionally taxing process of reflection, we have to be very clear about our assumptions and belief systems, so as to outlive the taxing period and be ready to enjoy the benefits of integrating reflection in our pedagogy, in terms of increased student learning and our professional satisfaction.

CHAPTER 4

Reflection

Some Models and Perspectives

Reflection is a type of thinking, associated with deep thought, aimed at achieving better understanding. There are several different models of reflection. Although they may vary in form and structure, they share some common features. The process of reflection begins with a description or acknowledgement of what has happened. This makes one realise, what is worth reflecting upon. It cannot be equated with mere observation, as critical thinking is inseparable from the process of reflection. It is followed by recognition, awareness and, finally, the changes required. Models can be referred to as frameworks of reflection, as they provide a structure to the process of reflection, though there can be no right or one way of reflection. For a teacher, it is important that he/she chooses the model which best suits his/her situation, since pre-service teachers are encouraged to reflect upon their teaching practices regularly. Here, we will discuss four models of reflections: Gibbs', John's, Kolb's and Driscoll's. After that, the insights gained from open-ended interviews, with practising teachers, would be discussed. They were asked questions, such as, what did they understand from 'reflection'; if and how they practised it; what, according to them, is the need and importance of reflection and so on. These four models of reflection are explained in this chapter, and discussed with the participating teachers, as well. Later, they were asked to comment on the merits and demerits of these models.

1. Models of Reflection

(i) Gibbs' Model of Reflection

Source: G. Gibbs. 1988. Learning by Doing

Graham Gibbs developed and based his reflective cycle, upon each stage of Kolb's experiential cycle (Kolb, 1984). He suggested that for a

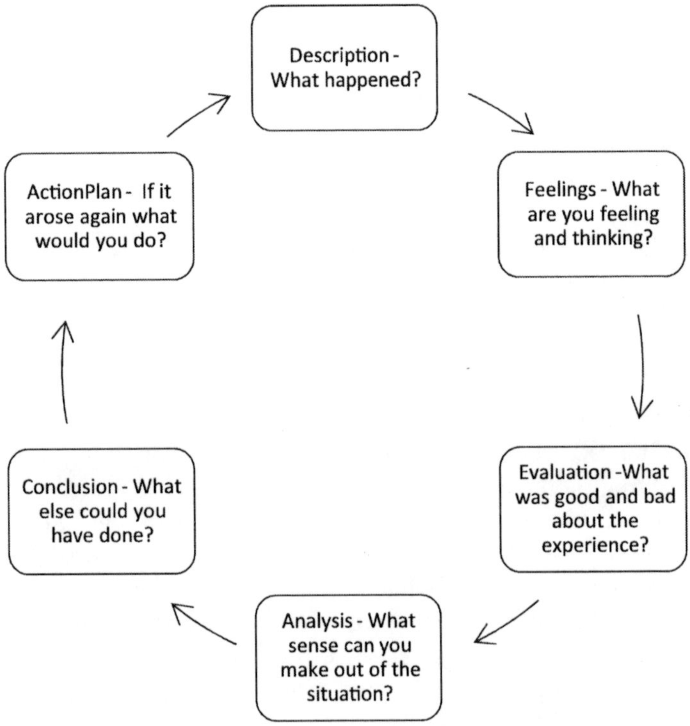

Fig. 4.1

fully structured analysis, the situation could be carried out, by asking prompt questions at each stage. The above given cycle can be illustrated as follows:

Questions to be considered at each stage of Gibbs' cycle

Description: Description tells us about what has happened. One is required to give a concise, factual account of the happenings. One is to provide relevant details and aims with which certain exercises had been undertaken. The aim is to make the reader aware of every detail of the event.

Feelings: One needs to identify and examine reactions, feelings and thoughts experienced at that particular time. It is important, although often difficult, to be honest about these. Here, one needs to explain her/his feelings and if they have changed since then. One has to make a record of the way their thoughts and feelings have affected their actions.

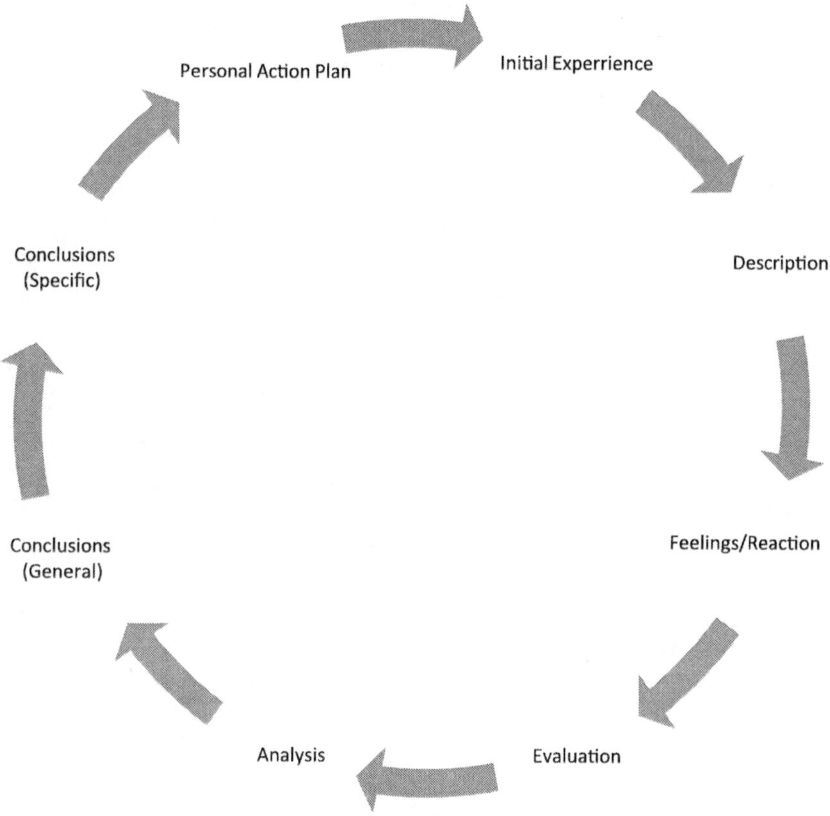

Fig. 4.2

Evaluation: For evaluation, one needs to look at the judgements made at the time, on how things were proceeding. One needs to consider the positive and negative aspects and what makes them so. For this, one needs to stand back from the experience, to gain a sense of how it went. One needs to be able to substantiate why they deem particular aspects as good or bad. One needs to examine their own judgements, what contributed to them, and how does one feel about them now.

Analysis: In this section of the reflection, one needs to examine the experience in depth, and start to theorise about key aspects and try to identify an overarching issue, or key aspect of the experience that affected it profoundly, which needs to be examined in future. For example, an aspect of communication or time management might have played a central part in the outcome. One needs to analyse how a situation can be worked out, in a better way, for the next time and the reason behind something's failure.

S/he would be required to question the ideas or theories one is aware of, how the theory about this aspect helps one make more sense of what happened, and how one could use this theory to improve this aspect in future. In this section, one needs to fully examine and make sense of factors affecting the situation and exploring ways to change and develop these.

Conclusion: To sum up are the key things learned through the reflective process, the main factors affecting the situation, and what needs to improve. This section might include naming specific skills that need developing, or aspects of organisation to improve. One might identify new knowledge or training which is needed.

Action plan: This should be the practical section of the process of reflection. One needs to think of ways one could do things differently the next time and how to prepare for this. The areas that need developing or thinking and the resources required need to be thought of. It is important to chart down the sequence of steps taken to improve one's practice.

During the interviews with some practising teachers, it was discovered that most of them found this model extremely feasible, in terms of its applicability. One of the teachers, when asked if she would like to alter the model, suggested a change, on the basis of her experience. It was experienced that the inclusion of "influencing factors" from John's model would make this model more comprehensive. She said that the 'influencing factors' should come after 'feelings'. All of them found it clear and easy to implement.

(ii) Johns' Model of Structured Reflection

Source: Johns, C. (1994). Nuances of Reflection. *Journal of Clinical Nursing* 3, pp. 71–75

Johns' model for structured reflection can be used as a guide for analysis of a critical incident or general reflection on experience. This would be useful for complex decision-making and analysis. He supports the need for the learner to work with a supervisor, throughout their learning experience. He refers to this as guided reflection. He recommends that students use a structured diary. Johns considered that, through sharing reflections on learning experiences, greater understanding of those experiences could be achieved, than by reflection as a lone exercise. He designed his model for structured reflection, through analysing the dialogue between those who were practising reflection and their guides who worked with them, throughout the learning experiences. Johns' model is based on five cue questions, which enable one to break down one's experience and reflect on the process and outcomes.

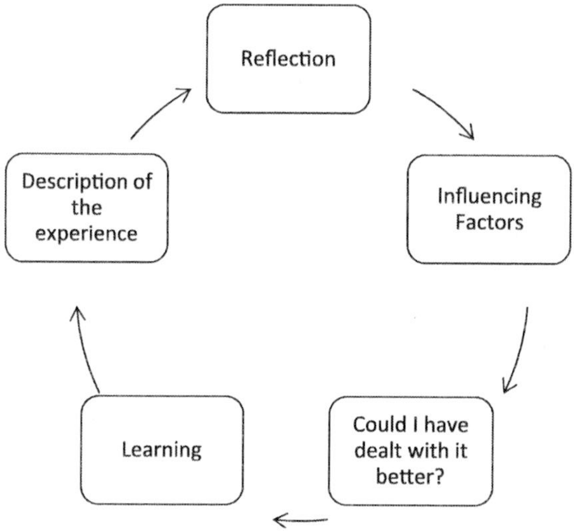

Fig. 4.4

Johns used Barbara Carper's patterns of knowing, in his model, which includes the following: aesthetics (the art of what we do), personal (self-awareness), ethics (moral knowledge) and empirics (scientific knowledge). To this model, Johns added the dimension of connecting the knowledge of previous experiences.

Description of the Experience: Give description of the experience and the significant factors. Also, chart out the key issues to which one needs to pay attention.

Reflection: Here, one needs to think of the aspects one was trying to achieve, along with its consequences.

Influencing factors: It refers to internal and external factors and sources of knowledge that affect the process of decision-making.

Could one have dealt with it better: It refers to the other choices that one has or not and their consequences.

Learning: It refers to the awareness of the ways in which one can make sense of the whole experience, in light of the past experiences and future practice. One needs to realise the changes that were brought about because of the experience and how one feels about them. One needs to recognise the ways in which the experience has changed one's way of knowing empirics – scientific knowledge, ethics – moral knowledge, personal – self-awareness, aesthetics – the art of what one does.

Most of the teachers found this model simple and easy to understand. But they preferred Gibb's model over it. They felt that the step involving 'influencing factors' was very significant, as it would help the teacher to analyse one's own sources of knowledge, that led to certain decisions. It was felt that this step could help them in the realisation of their biases and prejudices. One of the teachers said, "I can work towards being unbiased or unprejudiced only when I know what are the things towards which I'm biased and why."

(iii) Kolb's Learning Cycle (1984)

Kolb's learning cycle is a four-stage cycle. It applies to the way people learn through experience. The four stages include:

Concrete Experience: which is about a situation taking place.

Reflective Observation is a description of what happened. It, also, involves how one was feeling at that time.

Abstract Conceptualisation: questioning why it occurred and what could have been done otherwise, in order to prevent what was not good enough.

Active Experimentation or Testing Implications involves planning/practising concepts which were developed at stage three, so that, when the concrete experience occurs again, one may take a different action.

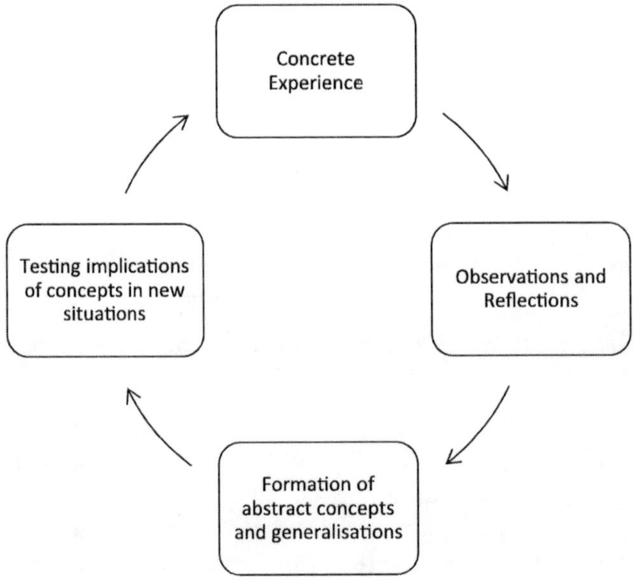

Fig. 4.5

Most of the teachers found this method very simple, but, less useful. Their argument for liking this method was its four-step process, which is simple and adaptable. Some of them said that in this model there are many experiences not as concrete as expected. Should one leave such experiences aside? Some mentioned that, at times, they felt certain things unconsciously and these feelings played a significant role in the reflection process. One said the second and first steps should be merged, in order that feelings and concrete observations could also be merged. The testing part was unclear to the teachers and they saw it as an evaluation process of the last three steps and, hence, did not agree with the fourth step. They said if, ultimately, we evaluate, where is reflection? They consider refection as a very subjective process.

(iv) Driscoll (by Borton) (2000)

John Driscoll developed Terry Borton's, 1970, three stem questions: 'What?', 'So What?' and ‹Now What?› in 1994, 2000 and 2007. Driscoll matched the three questions to the stage of the experiential learning cycle and added trigger questions that could be used to complete the cycle.

Stage 1- What: Returning to the situation: Here, one needs to describe what has happened, the incident one is reflecting upon and the facts or details of the whole event.

Stage 2- So What: Understanding the context: It refers to the understanding of the reasons which make an issue worthy of reflection. In this section, one researches the best practice/codes of conduct and so on and compares what happened against what should have happened.

Stage 3 - Now What: Modifying future outcomes: This step requires one to think of ways in which one might practise it differently in future. One is also required to think about how one would act or feel in the same situation in future.

The teachers said that they found this model to be the least useful and employable. They preferred Gibb's model over it. They said this model seemed to be incomplete, as lots of dimensions were missing.

2. Proposing a New Model of Reflection

During and after the interviews, it was found that, except for a few teachers, most of them were not conscious of the fact that they were practising reflection. Only after much probing, did they realise that reflection had been a part of their teaching process all along, whether in an organised or unorganised form. One of the teachers said that reflection is important in order to grow as a teacher and improve one's practices. It contextualises the teaching-learning process. Most of them agreed that they do 'spontaneous modification', while teaching. It was used when they felt that students were not responding in a desired manner or were not taking interest. One of them said that he did not think about the classroom processes outside the classroom. But, at the end of the discussions, he realised that reflection is not just about sitting on a table with a pen and diary and recording one's routine. He found that thinking about what went wrong in the classroom in the bus, on his way back home from school, was also reflection. One of the teachers said that reflection means thinking about the positives and negatives of one's teaching process. This thinking should lead to new ideas, which should be implemented. She felt that reflection is incomplete, if it does not lead one towards implementation of a new action plan. She continued that it should not stop there, as one needs to assess the comparative success of the new plan, as well. One of them opined that students' reactions help him to understand, if something is not going well with them. He said it is important to share a good rapport with one's students' and that students' input enriches the process of reflection. Another teacher stated that it is important to connect one's past experiences with the present and compare them in terms of development or deterioration. One should consider one's experiences as a student, while teaching. A teacher should never forget his/her experience as a student. This could help them in analysing students' expectations from them. One of them felt that inter-subjectivity and self-criticism are important aspects of being reflective. It was believed that students' input should be taken into account, while analysing one's classroom experiences.

After the interviews, a new model of reflection emerged, which is explained further with the help of a diagram.

Here, experience includes three things: the experience of the teacher, the experience of the teacher as a student in the past, and the experience of students. Thinking about these experiences, leads to reflection, where the teacher assesses the positive and negatives of an experience. With regard to this, one teacher maintained that this reflection would differ for each teacher, as they set goals for every class individually.

The next step is analysis. They felt that no two analyses could be the same. It is important to critically examine everything at this point. The next step is chalking out the feasible changes and their pros and cons, which leads to implementation. The process of reflection should not stop

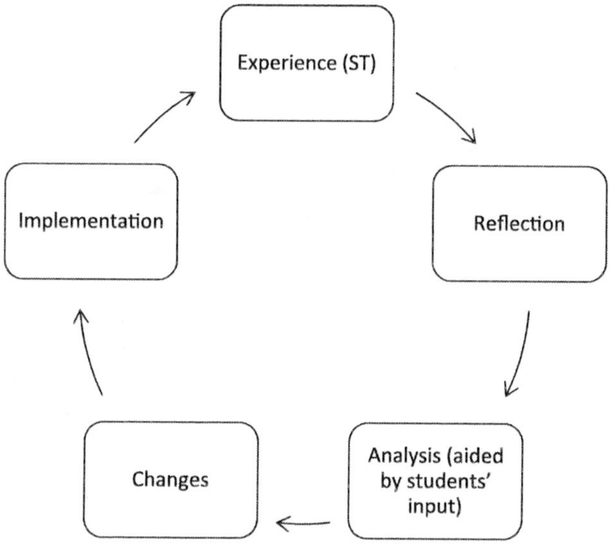

Fig. 4.6

here. The implementation of changes is a new experience, which further leads to the same cycle. This process should never end or stop. It is true that there cannot be one perfect model of reflection. One, constantly, needs to work with different models to find out which one would be better suitable for each teacher. Reflection is a subjective process, thus, it varies from person to person. Critical thinking and emergence of a more effective teaching practice are inseparable parts of reflection in teaching.

CHAPTER 5

A Teacher's Struggle

In the constant endeavour of meeting the expectations of the ideals of this noble profession, an average teacher, of whom we all have fond memories of our school days, faces near extinction in the current environment. In this research, it is tried to look at the world around him, through his eyes.

In the current setup of 100 crore movies to 100 per cent cut offs for admission, there has been a great deal of discussion on pressures on students, but we have to acknowledge the changing paradigms in a teacher's world.

First of all, let us be very clear on the nature of teaching, whether it is a profession, vocation or both or something hybrid. The *Oxford Dictionary* describes it as: a paid occupation, especially one that involves prolonged training and a formal qualification. A body of people engaged in a particular profession.

Vocation: a strong feeling of suitability for a particular career or occupation:

- a person's employment or main occupation especially regarded as worthy and requiring dedication.
- a trade or profession.

In the Indian context, where teaching has never been able to be just a profession and a teacher is expected to be seated on a pedestal as a 'guru', in terms of his effort, time and dedication, the expectations from a teacher have been converted to being lowly, such as a paid labourer, who has to perform to all the whims and wishes of his employers, without choice.

Actually, the teacher's professional status is quite debatable, as teachers tend to assert that they are professionals and entitled to all the benefits accrued to professionals. On the other hand, what is missing is the understanding of what teachers really do, need to do and be able to do, in understanding the elements of teaching as an occupation and teacher education as an occupational preparation. This is due to a lack of a clear and coherent definition of what we really mean by professionalism, which has had a significant impact on educational reform.

Richardson and Placier noted, 'teacher professionalism motivated a number of recent reforms, the outcomes of which are disputable because different versions of the supposedly same reform and multiple conflicting definition of 'professionalism'.

It is important to note here that we are concerned, principally, with professionalism, rather than professionalisation. The former refers to the internal works of the profession and the concern of a profession's members to do the best possible job for their clients; while the latter refers to external criteria such as status, salary specialisation and their control.

Millerson (1964) suggested that the characteristics that distinguished professions from other kinds of work included:

- The use of skills based on theoretical knowledge
- Education in these skills
- Examination to ensure competence in these skills
- A code of professional conduct, oriented toward the public good
- Professional organisation

  And a more recent and normative model by Shulman, 1990, suggests six common places, that are common to all professions:
  - ✓ Service to society, implying an ethical and moral commitment to the client
  - ✓ A body of scholarly knowledge that forms the basis of the entitlement to practice
  - ✓ Engagement in practical action, hence the need to enact knowledge in practice
  - ✓ Uncertainty caused by the different needs of clients and the non-routine nature of problems, hence the need to develop judgement in applying knowledge.
  - ✓ The importance of experience in developing practice, hence the need to learn by reflecting on one's practice and its outcome
  - ✓ The development of a professional community that aggregates and shares knowledge and develop professional standards.

This model of teacher professionalism is inward looking and focuses on critical reflective practice, i.e. the teaching profession should be understood not only as intellectual, but as a critical intellectual undertaking (Giroux, 1988).

Professionalism should be understood as a 'social construct'

To assume that the conception of 'profession' is context free and absolute, irrespective of societal values and morals, is problematic. As Thomas Popkewitz has noted, 'the term profession is a socially constructed word which changes in relationship to the social conditions in which people use it. Further, the word has no fixed definition or some universal idea, irrespective of time or place'.

In short, when discussing 'professions' and 'professionalism', we are, in fact, discussing the social status determined by a wide variety of factors, having little, if anything, to do with the innate nature of the occupation. It is because of this, that some educators and teachers may wish to be considered to be 'professionals'.

Finally, it could be described, through logical arguments, not particularly based on empirical evidence. (Reagon, T., *The Professional Status of Teaching*) as:

- A subject matter knowledge base
- A knowledge base, with respect to pedagogical knowledge
- A practical and experiential knowledge base, grounded in classroom practice
- Both personal and collective authority, with respect to issues of curriculum, assessment, and other policy and decision-making matters
- A meaningful career ladder, once one has been admitted to the profession
- A code of ethics for the profession, that is enforced by the members of the profession; and
- Commitment to ongoing personal and professional development.

The normative value attached to the word 'professionalism' cannot be denied. Generally, we do not speak of professionalism, as we do of unprofessionalism, i.e. we normally use these concepts, not so much to produce a positive norm of accepted beliefs but, in actuality, what is not accepted for educators/teachers.

In this study, discussion has been done with teachers of different backgrounds and setups, such as, a teacher teaching in a government school, a secondary teacher teaching in a private school run by a trust, a primary teacher in a government primary school. Apart from some common themes, which emerged in my detailed discussions about their profession, career, and in general, the problems they faced while teaching and their ways of tackling and coping, one thing which has emerged quite clearly and undisputedly is that teachers are a 'frustrated' lot. A lot of anger and helplessness against the system, administration and society at large, have crept into the teacher's psyche, which has, unfortunately, resulted in dilution of quality of interaction with students, which is, by far, the main motto of every teacher interviewed in this study.

It is not that teachers are not aware of this paradigmatic change in their outlook for the teaching profession, but this guilt has added to the frustration. The ways and mechanisms that are available to a teacher is dependent on his/her 'passion for teaching', which is, unfortunately, not a given and constant thing and diminishes with the passage of time and pressures (in most cases, unnecessary). Almost all the participants reported a loss in the amount of quality and meaningful time devoted to their teaching and students. The study has tried to understand this change and the varied reasons behind it.

According to the Health and Safety Executive figures, teaching is the occupation with the third highest amount of work-related stress (Smith, 2000).

The term 'job satisfaction' was first utilised by Hoppock, 1935, referring to a combination of psychological, physiological and environmental circumstances, that make a person feel satisfied with their job. The importance of being satisfied with one's job is captured in a quote by Darboe, 2003, as according to him, 'a job is not merely life-sustaining, but life-enhancing and enriching, because most people continue to work even if their economic needs are met, suggesting that, for most people, work satisfies various needs, such as a need for individual recognition, achievement, or the pleasure derived from working with other people' (ibid.: 84). The existing research, on job satisfaction, explores a variety of teacher background and school level factors that impact on the teachers' experiences in their work environment ... prolonged dissatisfaction with one's job may lead to teacher stress. According to Kyriacou, 2001, 'teacher stress may be defined as the experience by a teacher of unpleasant, negative emotions, such as anger, anxiety, tension, frustration or depression, resulting from some aspect of their work as a teacher' (ibid.: 28). Teacher stress can, also, involve a negative emotional experience, associated with the level of pressure and demands made on an individual, as well as the degree of mismatch between these demands and his/her ability to cope with them. Teacher stress can lead to strain (a reaction to stress) and teacher burnout (a state of emotional, physical and attitudinal exhaustion) (Kyriacou, 2001).

Teachers' job satisfaction and stress can have both economic and personal implications, as it can lead to stress-related employee absenteeism, burnout and a negative impact on pupil outcomes (Kyriacou, 1987).

An Irish study, by Merike Darmody and Emer Smyth, tried to find the factors associated with job satisfaction and occupational stress among primary teachers, the main sources of stress facing teachers teaching pupils who lack motivation; maintaining discipline; time pressures and workload; coping with change; being evaluated by others; dealings with colleagues; self-esteem and status; administration and management; role conflict and ambiguity; and poor working conditions. They found three types of factors exclusively:

- Micro level factors: the teachers' background such as, age, gender, length of service.
- Meso level factors: school level factors, such as school, teacher and student domains
- Macro level factors: salary, Government policies, professional status.

A study by Ololube, 2005, assessed the relationship between the level of teachers' job satisfaction, motivation and their teaching performance in Rivers State, Nigeria. The survey results revealed that teacher dissatisfaction was associated with educational policies, administration, pay and fringe benefits, material rewards and advancement. A study by Perrie and Baker, 1997, found that salary and benefits did not seem to have an impact on teacher satisfaction with their job.

Kyriacou, 2001, observes that, due to variation between countries and national education systems, there are differences in the main sources of teacher stress. He observes that job satisfaction is a complex issue in that 'even in the context of feeling overloaded, taking on additional duties in a valued area of work need not create more stress, and may indeed enhance job satisfaction'. *Smith and Bourke, 2002,* in Australia, explored work-related stress and job satisfaction among secondary school teachers and identified four aspects of teacher stress: staff tensions and conflict, time pressure, students and classroom conditions, and lack of rewards and recognition. Teaching context, workload and satisfaction were found to directly affect stress.

The study focused on generic occupational stress, teaching-specific stress, physical work environment stress and life events (measurement of non-work stress). The author found that teachers, studied in the sample, spend more than 55 hours per week, which is, much more than the standard 40-44 hours per week, as in the USA, which has a standard of 33 job hours per week. However, it is not just the quantity of time spent at school, but inadequate facilities were strongly associated as sources of stress. In terms of generic occupational stress, the five highest scoring items were: workload, insufficient resources with which to work, being undervalued, equipment, and not being able to switch off at home.

Teaching-specific stress was associated with lack of time spent with individual pupils, large classes, noisy pupils, difficult classes, and pupil motivation. The top ten sources of self-reported stress included: the pupil-teacher ratio, discipline, pupil motivation, inadequate resources, lack of parental support, teaching groups of differing ability, workload, parental expectations, salary, supervision/covering for absent teachers, and *demands on after-school time.*

The key roles of a teacher:

1) Learning specialist
2) Counsellor
3) Administrator
4) Moral guardian.

Here, it is tried to relate the following roles to the experiences of teachers i.e. their side of the story on the issues crucial for them. First of all, as the one responsible for students' learning, the list of challenges start with the obscene number of students in schools. The teacher in a private school is much better off than one in a government school, as it is observed that the teacher to pupil ratio in a government school is sometimes above 100 students in a class. Then, the question of learning or teaching gets lost and is, literally, thrown out and becomes just a matter of managing students. This problem is not only present in higher classes but, apparently, in primary classes, too. This has led to apathy among primary teachers. Though they understand the importance of personal interaction with pupils, they cannot do anything, apart from playing the role of a nanny to the children. The foundation of concepts and the general outlook of students does not become a visible concern for a primary teacher and the provision of the midday meal has added yet another layer of mismanagement. He/she has, now, to take care of the midday meal distribution. The duration of teaching time has added yet another constraint.

It is not that secondary teachers do not have to face similar time constraints. The sheer number of students in a class and their management, where the seating facilities are not available for even half the number, is a daunting task. Almost the entire first period is spent in just taking attendance and resolving daily issues. The challenges in a co-ed school, vis a vis a boys school, has unique dynamics. The teacher, with 15 years of teaching experience, notes these changes. Today, adolescents are restless, as the amount of exposure they have, at such a young age, poses problems in handling themselves, a feat in itself. You cannot expect them to be quiet or reasonable to allow a teacher to even start the proceedings. Thus, it is crucial for teachers to acknowledge their varied dynamic selves and, then, importantly, given them the required space, but how can that be achieved? A teacher threw this question back at me that how do you expect to give emotional, mental, personal space to each student in a class, where you cannot arrange the physical space for them to sit properly? Managing students has become such a prime concern in today's classroom that acknowledging the student's views, opinions and giving him/her space in classroom interaction, is a fundamental step for communication i.e. literally, the teaching-learning process never comes to the teacher's mind. For effective management, the pedagogical practices shift from 'regulation' to 'control'. The teacher interviewed admitted that her major guilt is that 'you have to be rough with children', though deep down she does not believe in scolding or physical punishment.

The issue now shifts to teaching concepts, where the teacher, at each level, blames the earlier teacher for not having done enough in preparing the child's basic foundation. As a result, whatever little time one gets, he/she has to start from scratch and faces the problem of uninterested students.

A particularly important observation made by a teacher was the unique challenge in teaching in dynamic cities such as Delhi, as students come from a wide range of cultural, linguistic and economic backgrounds to class and these differences are not only important for teachers and educators to manage the class, in terms of learning, but have to have awareness of these differences in the students. He observed that students form groups based on their region, language, dialect and so on. This initial differentiation among students is not bridged by the schooling process, but, is in fact, amplified. This bridging of socially constructed differences should be considered an important aim of democratic education, which is the aim of all our policy documents.

The teachers' realities in covering up these gaps is not just a theoretical exercise or paperwork but relates to moral dignity where this moral dilemma needs to be given due consideration and acknowledgment.

Minogue, 1973, *Chapter 4* suggests a reason for this by drawing a useful distinction between the academic and practical worlds. The academic world is one in which opposing theories continually battle with each other, isolated from practical pressures about what to do here and now. As he says, in the academic world 'no one has to come to a conclusion upon which a decision must be based'. In the practical world, decisions have to be made under different pressures, including the pressure of time. These pressures generate beliefs, involving simplifications, approximations and even working hypotheses that are known to be untrue, whose justification owes more to their efficacy, vis-a-vis action, and less to truth, to an extent not seen in the academic world. This is to say, that the goals sought by those in the academic world and by those in the practical world, may diverge considerably.

The private teacher, too, faces the problem of numbers, but she reminded the variations in the difference of parental/family support for students. The cultural, economic, regional differences play an important role in the students' learning experiences. This difference is observed in two incidents narrated by teachers. A teacher interviewed in a government school gave an account of an incident in his school, when a young teacher disturbed by abruptness and mischief of a particular student in class, tried to make him stand outside. The student refused to go outside class and when he did, he called the police PCR van to the school and the family nearly filed a police case against the teacher, for manhandling students. The family was unwilling to even listen to the teacher's side of the story and were ready to get the teacher arrested. It is not to comment on what was wrong and whose mistake it was, but the involvement of the police surely shows us what the teaching profession holds in today's India. Following this incident, what message has the family given to the student? That the teacher has no agency (or even status) in front of him. He could be bogged down by bureaucracy and influence i.e. he does not have any independent existence.

The other incidence was when, in a parent-teacher meeting, a parent started to beat his child in front of everyone, for performing poorly in examination. In this case, the teacher had to intervene to shield the child and, literally, scolded the parents for not knowing how to raise a child and asked them to leave the child in her guidance. In this situation, the family has shown that a child has no place of his own. Imagine the emotional trauma anadolescence has to go through with his family, when he should have relied on them for support. How can one imagine that a child will focus on learning and get his priorities right?

The negative attitude of parents towards schooling and students, has been identified as one of the important factors for this status quo. This is particularly true for government schools. The class difference is evident in forming attitudes and norms. For instance, the event where the student run away from school, without informing his teachers is very common these days and the school authorities ignore this issue. The responsibility of preventing indiscipline is more institutional than moral. The teacher has two options here: fight alone, which includes informing parents, counselling students and so on or hang up his/her boots and prevent him/herself from all this emotional trauma.

Even for the role of a counsellor, someone to whom a student can confide his/her problems, requires freedom, authority, time and institutional support to build that trust. A conscious teacher feels that he/she is working in a vacuum or running on a reverse escalator, i.e. whatever he/she tries, he/she does not seem to get anywhere.

Another important issue that needs critical review is the extra academic duties routinely endorsed by teachers. The government's approach towards the teaching profession is paid labour, whose maximum utilisation has to be seen in terms of 'physical resource', not as a 'intellectual resource' (*Teachers As Transformatory Intellectuals*, Giroux, 1988) which is the root cause of their societal status eroding. We cannot completely deny, at this stage of our understanding, that this approach towards teaching is not political or ideological, therefore, it definitely needs a critical discussion on our part to engage in this deconstruction.

The teacher gets to acknowledge that dialogue regarding learning and teaching is shaped, more broadly, by the educational policy and global capitalism and not just the teacher's immediate surroundings.

The fact that the teacher's job is relentless, is particularly stressful. Most teachers have little or no time between lessons to prepare, plan or simply recover. 'There is no breathing space,' one of the teachers said. If you have a bad lesson with a bad class, you don't get a chance to wind down.

Teachers do not get enough time to prepare lesson and, therefore, they take it up at the last moment. They hardly get time to prepare lessons, along with the other paperwork they have to complete. Although teachers enjoy longer holidays than most people, they, frequently, take the first week to recover and the last week to plan ahead.

A teacher said that they have to work for hours, which is simply ridiculous. Another teacher stated, 'I suppose, what makes it more stressful is the work often not directly related to the job.'

Organised reflection and reflection journals play the role of a pressure valve, as a pillar of hope and as something positive for teachers. Often, in this pressure cooker condition, the direction to proceed lies in analysing action and interphase with beliefs (knowledge).

Conclusion

Teacher job satisfaction and stress can have both economic and personal implications, as it can lead to stress-related employee absenteeism, burn out and a negative impact on pupil outcomes (Kyriacou, 1987).

From being respected and revered members of the community, teachers have moved into roles of disempowered government functionaries, relegated to the bottom few layers of the administrative hierarchy. Even as the pay scales of formal school-teachers have improved significantly, their accountability towards children and their parents has gone down. The pressure for universalisation, on the one hand, and a resource crunch on the other, has cleared the way for a new generation of teachers, who have since come to be known as para teachers, contract teachers, volunteer teachers.

The professional status of the teacher has gradually eroded not only for the community of stakeholders but also in the eyes of the teachers themselves, generating a sense of resigned cynicism in all sections of society.

Teacher autonomy, i.e., having a sense of control over their day-to-day teaching, particularly in deciding which age group they teach, is found to enhance job satisfaction and reduce stress. The main source of stress that was identified was the changing education policies of the government. Teachers' sense of control over various activities at school enhanced their job satisfaction, especially when they had a say in which class groups to teach. Teachers were also more satisfied when their students were well behaved, and their parents were more involved in school life. The composition and climate of the school was also an important factor of principal stress levels and satisfaction.

This study has emphasised one major point among others, which needs review, that teachers are not pushed to the wall where they have just two choices, either to erode his/her personal self in overcoming obstacles alone or just give up these all for his/her peace of mind. Important is that, we do not have to have either of those choices.

CHAPTER 6

Knowing About Knowing

This is an emerging field, where people try to know 'how they know', which comprises the field of personal epistemology. Lot of work has been done in this field across the disciplines, such as philosophy, sociology or psychology, yet when one tries to understand personal epistemology, one is faced with the question of what epistemological thinking and its process means and why it is essential. To do this, a comprehensive review of several epistemological work has been done, and the objective here is to elaborate upon the framework of epistemological development.

Ways of knowing are related to reflective inquiry, as reflective inquiry involves how one comes to know, how one learns and raises questions and, most importantly, how one becomes aware of oneself. Thus, how we perceive and understand knowing and knowledge has a relationship to inquiry, to explore and explain any problem or issue. It is important for a teacher to always try to understand how a student has discovered the processes of knowing and knowledge, their differences in this context and how this difference plays a major role in their learning.

This study has been conducted in phases. Special sessions were undertaken with students regarding "how to know what you know?" After this, written responses were asked in writing, on the work done with them. They appreciated the entire interaction. Some responses were really progressive, as they had learned a lot and had developed a tendency to think about most things, how they had come to know about these and what they know. However, some said it was a waste of time, as nothing actually helps in reality. Here, it is tried to make sense of these different kinds of responses and explore how students made sense of the long interaction held with them.

Constructing Understanding about Knowledge

The method chosen was very simple, where students were invited to participate in an interview at the end of their B.Ed. course. They were asked them about their experience of the last one year. It was assumed that most students' responses would relate to personality measures, revealing some aspect of their personality. But when their responses were analysed, it revealed that over a One-year B.Ed. course, students had undergone a radical change – important changes in the ways that they perceived knowledge, reality, authority and so on. It is tried to develop this model as a *scheme* of the students' capability to construct meanings. Over their course, students had been engaged in understanding coherent interpretive frameworks, re-knowing their ways of knowing, making meaning and taking decisions. All of this carried educational importance for understanding the teaching-learning processes.

Interaction was done with both types of students, those who were satisfied and those who were not with the interaction that was held with them, over a period of one year. Their responses helped me to conceptualise my understanding towards knowing. This analysis is developed into a few categories: *How do students develop process of meaning making and changing in the meaning over a period of time? What kind of duality are they faced with in this process? What kind of multiplicity has existed in this process? How can context help to develop understanding (contextual relativism) and what kind of commitment have they shown in the process of knowledge and knowing?*

The basic categories given above are taken as a loop, instead of a hierarchy. Why some were satisfied and why some not, is collectively being explained here. The responses show that there is a shift in the process, through which they perceived their way of knowing before interaction. They made it clear that it is not a matter of concern what they understand, what is important, is how they perceive this process of understanding and, thereby, meaning change. They achieved this understanding, through duality. Some students were known as freshmen before they began their educational careers, having a naive, dualistic perspective on knowledge and knowing, that is, they assumed all knowledge is known and that someone, usually an authoritative figure, knows the one right answer to any problem. As students developed, they came to realise that there are or can be multiple perspectives towards what is known and that many perspectives exist about what they know. They explored how these perspectives are different and how they are formulated. Understanding these multiple realities and truth helped them to develop a healthy perspective towards others. They realised that though there are multiple realities, some positions have a better grounding in evidence, than others.

Another component which kept working simultaneously was contextual relativism, where they tried to understand things in a specific context. They recognised that knowledge is situated in context and can be understood best only in that context.

The negative responses to the work went through this process of knowing but was slightly different. Some students could not see any use in the interaction had with them, which in their context, is also a kind of construction of knowledge as they went through the same process, where they discovered the meaning changing process, facing duality and challenges of multiplicity, wherein they situated this understanding in context. But, their responses were different from those who were satisfied.

It helps in realisation that all knowledge constructed has a relative stance or context. This contextual perspective is very crucial in the process of knowing. "Contextual relativism is the self-consciousness of being an active maker of meaning" (Moore 2002).

This entire change from the beginning to where they had reached was very radical and students achieve this through a transition process.

The revolution is both the most violent accommodation or representation of structure in the entire process of development and at the same time, the most calm. It involves a complete transposition between part and whole, and yet no student in my sample referred to it as a conscious event, a discrete experience, a 'realisation'. Once students had achieved this position of contextual relativism, they could not believe or acknowledge that they had ever held a dualistic one.

Like Piaget (a cognitive psychologist), author believes that change comes about for students, through their confrontation with different views on issues presented by peer students or their teachers. Informal discussions, conversations, challenging arguments, all serve to cultivate the process. Students themselves are the constructors of knowledge of these instances. We may call these different perspectives used for knowing.

There are two significant dynamics in the above discussion: (1) encounter and coping with diversity and ambivalence (uncertainty); and (2) the concomitant evolution of meaning-making about learning and self... as learners encounter levels of multiplicity, their meaning making transfers and evolves in predictable ways. Most importantly, knowledge is seen as increasingly speculative and uncertain, open to (and requiring) interpretation. This development triggers parallel shifts in a learner's views about the role of a teacher, as well as the role of a student.

This present sketch of epistemological development helped the author enormously in explaining about his students. It is important to know that the rich data collected of students' thinking and the change across their one year of the B.Ed. course has made the challenges faced by the students and their teachers understandable. It was discovered that people who faced challenges of revising their ideas and understanding of the world about knowledge and who or what could be trusted, might be obstructed by such changes and want to retreat or hold off accepting a new perspective. These could be sensible steps in their development. This research clearly brings forth a new discussion on adult development.

It has generated new research questions. Students of different liberal courses may show different ways of knowing, as sample in this research is restricted only to the B.Ed. course. Perhaps others are not privileged with the B.Ed. course structure and content. It was noted that students would often eagerly engage in argument when discovering that an opinion differed from theirs, trying to punch holes in it, because they are already graduates and have developed a sense of argument which may or may not be true with other graduate students.

But it can be effectively said that all knowledge is constructed by individuals themselves. It was kept in mind how different students came to understand themselves as students and knowers – not only how they viewed truth and knowledge, but also, how they saw themselves as knowers. Did they rely on others to hand them knowledge? Did they rely on their own "gut" feelings, or did they see themselves as users of procedures that could deliberately help to validate knowledge?

This concern to understand how these students made sense of their experience was focused on the procedures of knowing. Two major strands of procedures were identified: one, of trying hard to understand another's view, which the researcher called *"Connected Knowing"*; in contrast to another view, they termed *"Separate Knowing"* in which the individual self was to be kept at an objective stance, an evaluator, distanced from the position. The full scheme of the ways of knowing is indicated below:

How to know: Here, it would be good to discuss the ways of knowing, which will surely help teachers to know and understand the students' methods of understanding and knowing. We will be discussing about accepted knowing, subjective knowing, process oriented knowing, discrete knowing, joint knowing and constructed knowing.

Accepted knowing
The source of knowledge is external, locate in authorities which is accepted to know the truth. Truth can be actualized in words. Truth is one, complete, concrete, and accurate, so a thing is always right or wrong, true or false, good or bad. This may also be known as declarative knowledge.

Subjective knowing
The focus of knowledge is located in the individual. Listening to one's self becomes knowledge, seen as being based on individual experience and assumptions. There are many truths and multiple realities those exists simultaneously, and all are equally valid, but one's knowledge is fully right for me. Truth is personal and private and probably incommunicable and not transferable. this represnt constructive view of knowing.

Process oriented knowing
Knowledge is acquired and attained, developed, and communicated through the deliberate and systematic use of procedures.

Discrete and Apart mode
Focus is on analyzing and evaluating different views, understanding or arguments. Be abstract and analytic. Objectivity is achieved through being separate by adhering to non-personal standards and taking out one self from the process. Subjectivity is seen as non-healthy way of knowing. Basic objective is developing convinced truth.

Joint mode
Concentrating to understand and experience different perspectives and others' reality. Be storylike and comprehensive rather than debating and investigating. Objectivity is achieved through associations, accepting and assimilating another's perspective. Idea behind this is to construct meaning – to understand and be understood.

Constructed knowing
Constructed knowing
Knower is seen as active contractor of knowledge and knowledge is seen to be constructed. Use of both discrete and joint modes of discourse can become associated into a single approach or way of knowing, which includes contexts, out of which ideas emerges, and to take responsibility for developing systems of thinking processes. To learn about knowing and knowing about to learn.

CHAPTER 7

Knowledge Base for Continuous Professional Development

The last decade has seen a vast conceptual change in the professional development of teachers. Various institutions are associated with this work. These days, schools themselves take responsibility for the Continuous Professional Development of their teachers. But this is not true with regard to government school, as for them, State Council for Education Research and Training (SCERT), other agencies conduct orientation and refresher courses, claiming that they help in teachers' CPD. This claim, however, is open to inquiry.

It is a good innovative idea that professional development should be directly related to teachers' practices. It should be part of the school system on a regular basis, rather than something given by outside agencies over a period of time, annually. These CPD Programmes are curriculum based, such as the CPD programme for Social Science, Sciences and so on. That is how the entire scenario is continuously changing, but differently in private and government schools.

Past professional development (PD) practices had taken place without creating linkages with lived practices and mostly took place outside the school (though this is still in practice). These outside school programmes used to be very generic in nature and they just talked about general concerns about PD. They hardly dealt with subject-specific needs. Now the trend has changed, whether school-based or outside agency governed, PD programmes are based on subject specific needs, which somehow gives a better understanding to the teachers about PD in his/her related subject. Here, the teachers' attitude and perception is important. As we talked to many teachers during this project work, most of them (government teachers) said that these courses were hardly beneficial, and they do it because they have to do. The main reason behind the failure of this system was mentioned by teachers as being divorced from practice. Teachers said that usually whatever was taught to them was not applicable. Government brings policy changes without considering the realities and needs of the field and through these courses, the government expects policy implementation from teachers which is hardly possible.

PD, now largely known as CPD, should promote three things to help teachers for better classroom dealing. These are:

1) *Analysis of Practices*: Teachers need to know how to analyse classroom practices generally and specifically. Analysing may have many dimensions such as the relationship between teaching and learning and so on. This relationship can be general to a class and specific to a particular student's needs. Such analysis has been ignored by most PD programmes. They focus more on the outcome of classroom teaching, suggest small tricks for a better result, which really, does not help teachers in their CPD nor learners to learn better. Teachers need opportunities to analyse their own practices.
2) *Exposure to Alternatives*: Teachers must have alternatives to deal with the class, under all circumstances. This does not only include pedagogic instruments, but a perspective about teaching which is reflection based on analytical understanding.
3) *Decision regarding Methods*: Teachers must be equipped with the ability to choose/develop a method, according to the needs of the class and the concepts. This decision is based on analysis and looking at alternative practices. It is needed because teaching is very complex. Having knowledge and understanding of one way or practice cannot help for longer or will not help in sustainable CPD.

If we ask ourselves, what is a better form of professional development and what kind of practices are quality based practices, one will have various answers. But a good example can be seen as the in-service mentoring process, where pre-lesson discussion, class observation and post-lesson discussion for better teaching are involved. It provides space for teachers to share their ideas with each other, facilitating them in understanding their teaching from different perspectives. This seems to be good as there will be no supervision, the entire system will be school based and will work on a collective basis. Other forms of CPD programmes can be seen based on action research and reflective practices. But what is more important is that teachers should not be reluctant. Researches show that many teachers are reluctant to these changes and practices.

To overcome these challenges, there is need for some serious changes.

First, we are not equipped with sufficient knowledge for CPD, one of them is not having a knowledge base for CPD. The teachers learn individually from their experiences, but their learning is restricted only to them and there is no official way to share their experiences with other colleagues. But, generally, we depend on researches conducted by universities and other organisations which lack direct school experiences. Such researches alone, cannot develop a platform for teachers' CPD. We have to develop the approaches where lived practices are associated with other academic researches.

Second, we need an environment where such collaborative work can sustain in itself. It will never be sustainable if teachers keep considering it as extra work or work which can be done in their free time. Rather, it has to be looked at as work, which is prevalent and sustainablee in their regular routine.

Third, there are certain practical things teachers need to know, such as, the process of analysing practices, which hardly exists in our school system. Therefore, developing such culture will take time. For this, a knowledge base is needed and how this knowledge base for teaching and CPD can be created, is an important question to explore further. It is important to acknowledge that this knowledge base should be created by teachers, as this will help in their professional development. If we fail to develop such strength in teachers, we will surely fail to move ahead on this path and keep working on practices without any critical vision. In the next few years we will need such organised knowledge about CPD to develop a positive school ethos for CPD, and this knowledge base should be centralised in such a order that it could be accessed and shared by the whole teaching community.

Other important concern is that looking towards the Government all the times may not help the system; self-willingness and desire for development will open doors for required CPD. Moreover, sharing experiences consciously help in attaining the result.

Although it seems to be tough, but it is possible to build a platform where teachers can share things, ideas and experiences collaboratively with other colleagues, not only within the school but across the schools. This will put them on the path of CPD.

Technology is playing a major role these days in all sectors, including education. Yet, there are teachers who are uncomfortable with technology. We have to revisit the use of technology in education. The popular power point presentations (PPT) has been seen as using technology in education. There are other uses of technology in education and we have to research further with regard to this. For example, showing a video itself can be used effectively and can be used as pedagogy, but only if teachers and students are aware of what and how to observe and analyse observations. Thus, simply saying we need to use technology and making teachers literate about MS-Word etc., will hardly solve the purpose.

Another important aspect is to improve the quality of teaching. For that, we have to ensure that only those, who wish to be teachers, should enter the teaching profession. Teaching as a profession should be their choice and not by chance, because those who choose teaching as a profession by choice will be able to contribute more, instead of those who become teachers by chance. There is a need to improve the teachers' competence and perspective towards teaching and this is possible only with the collaboration among teachers.

The reality of the Indian school education system is that most students are taught by an average teacher, who uses average methodology. This fact cannot be denied. Therefore, what is needed is to improve this average methodology and bring it to the next level. This improvement will build up the teachers' competencies to a great extent.

Another issue important to highlight here is regarding the standard practice, i.e. teaching through a single method. Though, there is no harm in using a single method, but one should have the means to improve these standard practices. Professions, such as medicine, have developed tremendously in the last decade, not because more intelligent people go there, but because they manage to develop an environment of sharing practices, which is still missing in the teaching profession. This change in medicine has happened because of the knowledge base developed by the practitioners themselves which is, again, missing in the teaching profession. In case, if it is happening somewhere, it still needs to be improved.

Expecting too much from teachers is also wrong. They cannot do everything, as they also have limitations, but if they fail to do so, the system starts blaming them, which is incorrect. For better CPD, there are certain things which need to be focused upon. *First*, an effective, but soft administrator in school (principal), *second*, there should be more focus on learning, and *third*, maintaining practices, that are continuous and ongoing. This ongoing and persistent practice will show great sustainable results and create an environment and context, where everyone will be motivated to improve their practices, which will lead them towards their professional development.

CHAPTER 8

Reflective Practice

Process and Journal Writing

Learning comes from many different incidents and experiences that we have in life. We can learn much about ourselves, others, our job, our organisation, and professional practice, as well as our abilities and skills, if we consciously take out time to reflect on our learning. 'Learning' suggests ongoing action and perpetual curiosity. In Chinese, the term 'learning' is represented by two characters: the first means "to study", and the second means 'to practice constantly.' Many schools operate, as though their personnel know everything, they will ever need to know the day they enter the profession. The school that operates as a professional learning community recognises that its members must engage in the ongoing study and constant practice that characterises an organisation, committed to continuous improvement.

John Ruskin once wrote, '*Quality is not an accident. It is always the result of intelligent effort.*' Reflection is this process of intentionally focusing (intelligent) one's attention on a particular content; observing and clarifying this focus; and using other knowledge and cognitive processes (such as self-questioning, logical analysis and problem-solving) to make meaningful links. Self-reflection is a specific form of reflection in which the content for reflection is self-referenced to one's thoughts, feelings, behaviour or personal history.

Reflective practice is a process, which enables you to achieve a better understanding of yourself, your skills, competencies, knowledge and professional practice. Although most of us engage in thinking about experiences either before, during or after an event, we need to document our understanding, in order to clearly identify and demonstrate the components of our learning. Identifying what we have learnt requires us to think about our experiences, and consider the outcomes, in order to evaluate the experience, and identify our thoughts, feelings and understanding of the relevant issues. The objective is to identify what we have learnt, in order to construct new or different approaches to our future practice, or to recognise and validate effective practice to utilise in future.

Most teachers reflect on their performance in an informal way, but it is worth considering a more formal approach or model. This involves reflective practice, as part of a process called an action research cycle.

The teacher, as a reflective practitioner, 'is one who continually evaluates the effects of his/her choices and actions on others (students, parents, and other professionals in the learning community) and who actively seeks out opportunities to grow professionally." (Schon).

A reflective practitioner's knowledge includes an understanding of methods of inquiry for self-assessment and problem-solving, awareness of major areas of research on teaching and resources available for professional learning. A reflective practitioner's dispositions have been described as including a valuing of critical thinking and a commitment to continual learning and refining practices.

Dewey was one of the first philosophers to include reflection in his educational framework. He defines reflective thought as the 'active, persistent, and careful consideration of any belief or supposed form of knowledge in the light of the grounds that support it and the further conclusions to which it tends' (1933/1910).

Dewey states that it is necessary to develop the habit of reflective thinking and his reflective activity begins with an experienced obscurity, doubt, conflict or disturbance, and with setting of the problem. Next, an inferential leap to an idea for a solution is made. Then, a hypothesis is considered, elaborated and finally tested. Reflective thought is distinguished from mere mental streams because it is an ordered sequence of ideas that are really a 'consequence' of each other. *Thus, reflective thought is inquiry, it leads somewhere and there is a goal or conclusion to be reached.*

Schon believes there are some processes central to professional competence that cannot necessarily be taught or described through scientific theory or techniques. Instead, professionals think about what they are doing as they are doing it, in a process Schon labels it 'reflection-in-action'. Accordingly, when professionals are faced with a problematic situation, they delve into their repertoire of past experiences to frame the problem and look for new possibilities for action. Schon purports that reflective practitioners 'conduct and frame experiments in which they impose a kind of coherence on messy situations... that constitutes a reflective conversation with the materials of a situation – the design like artistry of professional practice.'

Reflective practice may be thought of as occurring on levels or stages. Max Van Manen (1977) claims that the practical use of educational knowledge occurs in an increasingly reflective manner and suggests there are three levels of reflection. His hierarchy of reflective thought begins with the technical level, where educational techniques are applied to attain a given end. However, Van Manen sees the next level, the interpretive, as being a more adequate way for teachers to make practical use of their own experiences in the reality of their classrooms. For the highest level, Van Manen (1977) looks to critical analysis and emancipation and notes 'the practical addresses itself, reflectively, to the question of the worth of knowledge and to the nature of the social conditions necessary for raising the question of worthwhileness in the first place'.

Another conception, that reflective practice occurs in stages, comes from Patricia M. King and Karen S. Kitchener's (1994) *seven-stage Reflective Judgment Model* which asserts that reflective judgment is developmental.

At the lower stages, knowledge is viewed as certain, and beliefs are justified because of direct observation, authority figures, or evidence. Idiosyncratic, contextual, and subjective knowledge and justifications occur in the middle stages.

King and Kitchener claim that truly reflective thinking occurs only at the upper stages, where knowledge is constructed from a variety of sources; 'knowledge is the outcome of a process of reasonable inquiry, in which solutions to ill-structured problems are constructed,' and 'beliefs are justified probabilistically, on the basis of a variety of interpretive consideration'.

Reflection in educational settings is a practice that facilitates the exploration, examination and understanding of what we are feeling, thinking and learning. It is a thoughtful consideration of academic material, personal experiences and interpersonal relationships. Reflection is a form of internal inquiry that extends the relevance of theory and deepens our understanding of the practice of our everyday life and work.

The role of systematic efforts in a reflective process is very crucial in reflection in educational settings. Journal writing and other techniques can offer a viable cue for satisfying and successful reflection.

Donald Schon (1930-1997) was responsible for the development of a number of remarkable contributions to understanding the theory and practice of learning. He was responsible for providing 'reflection' a valid status, as a legit mode of learning. He coined the phrases 'the learning society' and *'reflection-in-action'* and developed the concept of *reflective practice.* He argued that any organisation or community must learn in order to continue to develop and change, and to avoid threatening its basic functions. He introduced the idea of professionals becoming *reflective practitioners.*

We must become able, not only to transform our institutions, in response to changing situations and requirements; we must invent and develop institutions which are 'learning systems', that is to say, systems capable of bringing about their own continuing transformation.

Opportunities for teachers to evaluate themselves (*Reflect on own practice)* in schools are often few, and, usually, happen only in an informal manner. Action research can serve as a chance to really take a look at one's own teaching in a structured manner. While the focus of action research is, usually, the students, educators can also investigate what effect their teaching has on their students, how they could work better with other teachers, or ways of changing the whole school for the better. Conversations can take on a different focus, from attempting to 'fix', to arrive at understanding.

Action research as reflective practice is a form of teacher professional development and reflection, which allows teachers to grow and gain confidence in their work. Action research projects influence thinking skills, sense of efficacy, willingness to share and communicate, and attitudes toward the process of change. Through action research, teachers learn about themselves, their students, their colleagues, and can determine ways to continually improve. The practitioners can focus on school issues, problems, or areas of collective interest.

People have mental maps with regard to how to act in situations. This involves the way they plan, implement and review their actions. Furthermore, it is these maps that guide people's actions, rather than the theories they explicitly espouse. One way of making sense of this is to say that there is a split between theory and action.

After knowing all this, there is a possibility that we understand reflection mistakenly. Thus, it is important to understand, what reflection is and what it is not. The following diagrams explain this.

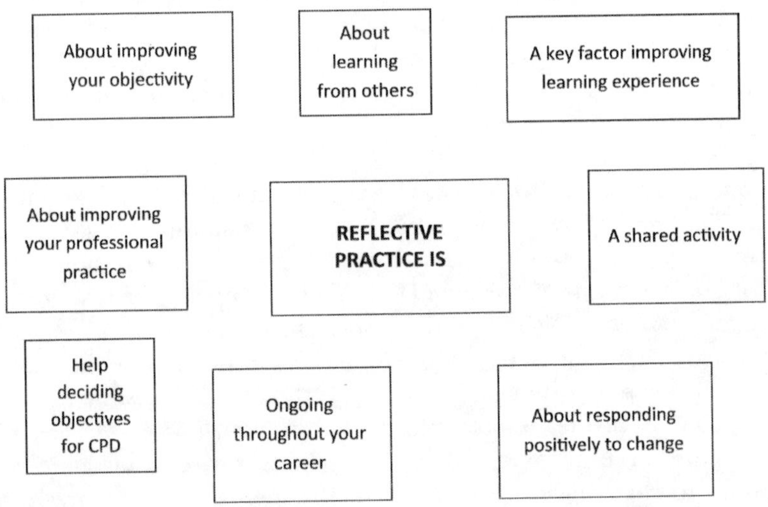

Fig 8.1

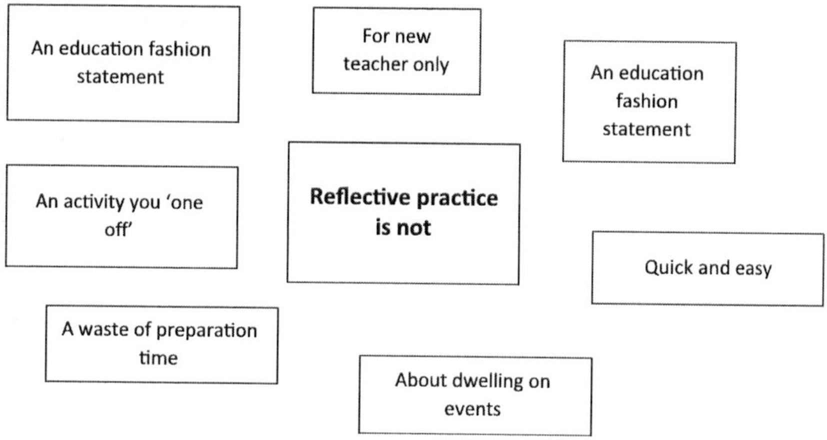

Fig 8.2

Routine deployment of specific procedures cannot, on its own, be expected to suffice for the achievement of purposes: 'what works' depends on the dynamically changing context. That is, unpredictability poses problems and problems require solving, which means conscious deliberation. It has to do more with including 'reflection' as an approach in one's work culture, than to practise some set of drills, focus on enjoying process than to achieve some product. That being said, some guides or starting clues to start this journey were presented.

Understanding and using reflection as a routine practice is a challenging but possible task, which involves one's own review and analysis. Very simple and meaningful questions to oneself can help to develop reflectively or as a reflective practitioner. Some such questions can include:

- What were the three most important things you learned last year and how did you learn them?
- How have you improved your value to learners and your school over the last 12 months?
- What aspects of your work have been changed by your continuing professional development in the last 12 months?
- How have you disseminated your learning over the last 12 months?
- What are the three main priorities for your continuing professional development in the next 12 months?
- What are the key differences you want to make for your learners and your school in the next 12 months?

- How will you plan to cater to your needs for continuing professional development over the next 12 months?
- When will you next review your needs for professional development?

To conclude, it can be said that knowing oneself is the beginning of becoming a good reflective practitioner.

Methods of Reflective Practice

Reflective practice can be formal, e.g. for a course, an overall review could be carried out. A less formal approach could simply involve the practitioners reflecting back on teaching experience and considering the various activities carried out as part of their teaching. Van Manen (1977) proposed technical, practical, and critical levels of reflection, and Grimmett, MacKinnon, Erickson, and Riecken (1990) observed three perspectives on reflection:

- *Prospective reflection*: reflection as instrumental mediation of action,
- *Reflection in action:* reflection as deliberating among competing views of teaching, and
- *Retrospective reflection:* reflection as a reconstructing experience. Although these three conceptualisations are not perfectly parallel, the dimensions applied in this article certainly are.

An important criterion of reflection differing from any other form of thought is 'continuity' (Dewey, 1910). A random act of retrospection or thinking about actions cannot be termed as reflection. Thus, it involves using a range of techniques and tools, over a period of time, for the purpose of 'meaning making', improving practices, professional growth and so on.

There are various techniques which can help in this reflective process:

- Keeping a *journal,* reflecting in writing, on the various training sessions delivered.
- *Critical incident analysis* is where key incidents, during the teaching, are analysed and evaluated. It is important to remember that this should involve positive events, as well as those where the training did not achieve its objectives.
- *Mind mapping* involves the practitioners in 'drawing' the ideas surrounding a particular concept or problem in the form of a 'mental map', allowing the trainer to reflect, clarify and reshape their ideas.

Reflective practice should not always be thought of as a solitary process, to be carried out by an individual trainer. It can be useful to involve others in the process:

- *Peer review* involves other trainers observing the training and providing their feedback.
- *Mentoring* involves using another, usually more experienced trainer, to act as an advisor.
- Identifying a *critical friend*: This individual is enlisted as a listener and 'sounding board' by the trainer.
- *Online training communities:* Technology now allows trainers, with common interests, to share problem-solving techniques and examples of good practice.
- PLC Professional Learning Communities (PLC) is a collaborative venture of like-minded professionals having shared goals, beliefs and aims to help each other to grow, by solving problems together, which they cannot solve alone.

Through reflection, we challenge our assumptions, ask new questions and try to make sense of our experiences. Instead of being passive receivers of external expert knowledge, we become active creators (and co-creators) of our own knowledge. As reflective learners, we test our informal theories (those that we develop through our experiences as practitioners in the world) against formal theories (those that are developed by researchers and academics). We integrate theory and practice through a process of reflection-on-action, i.e. trying to make sense of experience after the fact and reflection-in-action, i.e. trying to make sense of experience, while it is occurring (Schon, 1987).

In nutshell, one may choose the way or method s/he is comfortable with, but reflective journal is one of the most used and important methods of reflection.

Reflective Journals

Reflective journals is a crucial source or tool for reflection. It can serve as a source of data for analysis on teaching practices, its assumptions or providing references for actions, over space and time, by recording conversations and contemporary ideas, and uncover implicit belief systems for questioning and improving.

If one has not kept a reflective log, a diary, journal or sketchbook, one may have some questions about how to do it and why it can be useful for oneself. One may wonder about the purpose, as well as what it should look like. The teaching journal as a method of instructional improvement is recommended. Teaching journals can improve the teaching, not only of beginners, but also of experienced instructors.

Hobson (1996) calls the teaching journal a, 'textbook of emergent practice'. His list of teaching journal functions is largely comparative: a journal 'suggests questions, identifies new areas to explore, reveals meaningful absences, and uncovers recurring patterns.' Of all these, the comparative dimension of a teaching journal provides a way for instructors to compare their current practices against alternatives: other pedagogical approaches and theories, or simply new ideas for teaching a familiar course. Some of our best ideas for teaching a class, the second time, could come from the intellectual challenge of remembering and putting into words our impressions and interpretations of the content of a particular class meeting.

Why should we even keep a Reflective Journal?

Keeping a journal helps you to get in touch with your reactions to readings, behaviours, experimentation, cohort dialogue, work experiences, and interpersonal relationships. It will help you 'think about the way you think', encourage the integration of theory and practice, and serve as a record of your experiences and learning in the programme. It gives a perspective to our actions, and helps to de-contextualise our actions and behaviours and learning from it.

Keeping a journal and, more importantly, reading that journal, creates more accountability and preserves observations and ideas about teaching in order to benefit future students. It fosters an ability to observe what is happening in the classroom. The framework in which we situate our observation is fine-tuned, by our sustained practice of reflection. It provides us a theoretical background to situate our observations and thus be effectively analysed for maximum results. Used most effectively a journal is not just about reflection, but about reflection that leads to action, and action that creates improvement.

Sometimes, we do not feel enthusiastic for teaching. A quick read of past journal entries could reveal something from an earlier class that provides a new idea for a current class. Reading about past successes and lessons increases our energy level and helps us to look forward to teaching.

How to go about writing a Reflective Journal

A reflective journal is a personal expression of who you are, therefore, you will choose how it looks. Everyone has different qualities that make him or her unique. Therefore, a journal can take many different forms. It can be an electronic journal, a sketchbook, a notebook, a binder, an audiotape or a combination of some or all of these forms. A 'record' in it can include such things as written reflections, drawings, 'doodles', pictures, poems, colours, clippings, quotes, descriptions of dreams, double entry journaling and mind-mapping or branching. The benefits of each of the different forms or styles may only become apparent as you try them. You are encouraged to experiment with forms that you have not used before. You may find that through this process, certain forms open up more ideas, feelings, energy and creativity for you. You should not feel constrained or limited to one style. You may find that what works for you is a combination of different styles, or you may find that you lean toward a particular style, depending on your needs or feelings at the time. Journal keeping can be a lifelong process with many benefits. You may choose to continue to receive these benefits, even after your specific experiences are complete.

Ways of Journal Writing

There may be many ways of journal writing. A few of most common ways are:

Double-entry journals involve a two-step writing process (Hobson 1996; Risko, Roskos, and Vukelich 2002). The basic idea of any method of reflection (or even journal writing) is a systematic way of organising ideas (both implicit and explicit), to record them to be able to draw patterns and meaning and thus improve the instructional efficiency. Therefore, to fulfill the objective, you can use various patterns and style of recording.

For example, in double entry journals, you can use a binder or notebook, in which you can use each of the two facing pages for a specific purpose, the left-hand page to take notes from the readings and the right-hand page for your reflections. On the left, include the source of the reading, quotations that stand out, a summary of key points, steps or procedures, models or frameworks. Use the right-hand page for your reflections about the reading. You might include your responses to the material, how you are going to apply what you have read, any questions you have, something new you have learned. You can include points you agree with, ideas you disagree with, areas which were not clear, critiques of the clarity of the writing or the ideas presented. Be thoughtful in your comments – do more than say '*I liked the chapter*' or '*The chapter didn't make sense to me*'. Reflect on how the information fits with your current knowledge or experience. Ask yourself questions such as '*Did I learn something new?*', '*Do I agree or disagree with this author?*', '*What questions do I have for this author?*', '*What irritated me about this reading?*', '*What was helpful about this reading?* If you are keeping your journal on the computer, you could set up two columns to work with.

Of course, the benefits of being involved in journal writing depends on the rigour with which it was implemented. This process will encourage active, reflective learning, instead of passive memorising of information (or skimming over material). It allows you to engage with the reading as a form of dialogue, almost as though you were having a conversation with the author. The process helps you to clarify your thoughts and reactions and helps in preparing your online conversations. This does not mean that you have to have all the answers of your questions, puzzles or concerns before you go online.

The double-entry process helps you to extend your thinking about the reading, so that the online discussion can take place at a deeper level than simply saying you liked or did not like the article. Most importantly, the process will help you to link theory with practice. It encourages you to consider the ways in which theory can inform about your work and the ways in which your practical experience might inform about theory.

Stream of Consciousness Writing: It is a stream of ideas and thoughts, your spontaneous reaction and reasoning behind any action. It can help you to uncover your inherent belief system, assumptions and provides a healthy ground for a critical analysis. There is no need to limit yourself to a pattern or model, as it may hinder free flow of thoughts, which is the sole purpose of this style.

Write non-stop for a specified period of time or specified number of pages. Say to yourself, *'I will not stop writing, until I have filled three pages'* or *'I will write non-stop for 5-10 minutes.'* Write down anything that comes into your mind at the time of writing. Or talk non-stop into your tape recorder. Speak or write without censorship. Nothing is too 'silly' to write down or talk about. Do not look at your pages or listen to your tape with a critical perspective. The point is simply to come out in a concrete form the thoughts zooming in your mind at the time of recording. Do not feel that you have to re-visit what you have recorded for many days.

The exercise is very freeing. It stimulates your brain, removes the constant chatter or self-talking and helps to clarify your thoughts. The activity removes the control of the 'logic' or 'censoring' part of your brain and permits the more open 'artist' or 'creative' part of the brain to function. This is the part that makes connections between things that may not appear to be connected on the surface but do have relationships in your subconscious. These more 'hidden' connections sometimes, can show the way to the things that are troubling you or come out with creative solutions. By getting all the surface 'running around in circles' thoughts out of your brain, and onto the page, it frees your mind to function more efficiently. By getting more subconscious thoughts onto the page, you may discover (over time) clues to the true essence of what you are feeling, plus good suggestions and possible solutions to problems you have been trying to resolve.

Mind Mapping: It is a relatively new approach of journal writing. The process can have layers of complexity, but the basic rules of Mind Mapping are: to begin with a central image or picture that represents your topic; place this image in the center of the page which is lying horizontally; put key words that relate to your central image on lines that radiate out from the central image; limit yourself to one key word per line; print or draw your key words in a way that relate to their meaning and keep the length of the line close to the length of the word; put additional key words that relate to the previous key word in a declining slope, off the central radiating lines; use lots of colours, images, sizes, codes – whatever works for you to give the words greater association and meaning.

The benefits of this rigorous and slightly technical way are rather quick as it approaches visual senses. Patterns emerging out of ideas can be revolutionising and if performed earnestly, results can be unexpected.

Mind Mapping is a technique developed by Tony Buzan, as a form of associative note-taking that follows the natural patterns of the way your brain functions, in that the brain likes to make links or associations in a radiant manner, often referred to as Radiant Thinking. The mind-mapping technique also follows the pattern of interlinking neurons within the brain and the manner in which information is transmitted from neuron to neuron. The theory is that this style of recording helps the brain to work with greater clarity and to make more associations and connections, which improves learning and retention of information. The intention is to increase mental freedom and function. It is believed that this form of notetaking increases the input of information from both the left and right hemispheres of the brain, thus encouraging 'whole-brain' thinking.

One is free to combine/synthesise various type of journals described above, to modify according to one's needs and contexts. The flexibility it offers can be very rewarding. Also, as situations vary, being limited to any one style of writing can be, at times, a handicap.

There are other ways of using journals for facilitating 'reflective learning', such as, logs, reflective essays, peer observations, professional discussion and so on.

With all the ways and styles of journal writing, a core issue is how to do the *analysis* of one's own experiences and 'reflection' *per se.* One may use various techniques to do this task. Some such techniques are – to question, seek alternatives, keep an open mind, view things from different perspectives, ask 'what if', seeking, identifying and resolving problems. The most important aspect of reflective practice is the 'attitude' one has towards becoming a reflective practitioner. Suggested ways may not be helpful if attitude in not positive. So being critical with positive attitude is very important.

CHAPTER 9

Diary Writing

A Tool for Professional Development

Diary writing has become an important and very feasible way of CPD in the educational context. This technique has become popular, not only for language teachers, but for all disciplines. This technique has a more comprehensive use, even in teacher education. It is a reality that most of the work in diary writing is available in Language and not in other subject areas, like Science, Social Science and so on. Here, we examine the diary writing and experiences of four Social Science teachers which helped them to develop professionally and also to grow as active and reflective practitioners. They agreed to write diaries for six months. Some significant portions of the diaries are incorporated to elaborate upon the importance of diary writing for CPD.

Here, it is significant to introduce the context of the present work. The sample was taken from two government schools of West Delhi. With great difficulty, four teachers were made agreed to be part of the present work. Initially, they felt 'writing a diary' burdensome job, because they had to do it additionally along with their routine schoolwork. But, gradually, they started enjoying writing diaries.

The diary writing can be a tool for professional development has not been thought by most teachers, not even those who were part of this study, as they always viewed it as an extra burdened. Some of them have never thought that it could be a powerful way for their CPD. As mentioned in the box, they were not aware of the fact that simply writing diary can facilitate their professional development.

> *"it never came to my mind that only writing my experiences in a diary can help me to develop professionally......now, when I look back where I began, I am surprised and feel very ashamed, that why had I not started it before."*
>
> *From a teacher's diary*

It is important to mention that using diary as a tool for CPD and for one's own development and growth can become useful, only if the teachers are willing to do it by choice. Forcing them will not help in this process as reflection and reflective practices can only be self-developed. It is possible that some teachers do write diaries, but they do it just for the sake of doing it.

Diary writing does not have common benefits for all. Teachers may define their own benefits from diary writing. Some may find its benefits for pedagogy, some for classroom management and some at a larger level for their professional development. Diary writing is directly associated with reflective understanding. What and how a teacher involves his/her experiences in diary writing is crucial. Some may write only on classroom processes, some may also include corridor talks and other may even include other general observations which have been done by them unintentionally, such as during the assembly or something else happening on the playground. Hence, what a teacher will include and how this inclusion will benefit the teacher, is very subjective. This subjectivity can be strengthened according to the teachers' needs, as they will be different. Thus, the criticism of hardcore objectivity can be avoided here. That is how diary writing can be perceived, as a good tool for action research in class and for the teachers CPD.

We have to acknowledge that diary writing is an inherent part of the process or concept of teacher research, where it is used as a way of pedagogic reflection and CPD. What is expected from the teacher is to raise questions and issues about their own classroom practices, in order that they can reflect upon them and can think of possible solutions. In most of the nations, a lot has been done in this regard, but hardly any steps are taken in India. There is a great need to move towards a more active role for teachers in classroom research, where they work as active practitioners. Their own research will be more contributing, as it is being conducted in their own context. Teachers should not worry about its validity and being implemented in a larger context, because with such processes they will be able to resolve the problems on their own, as they all have their own specific history and meaning. Later, their researches can be seen on a larger educational spectrum.

Diary writing, as a process, can be done by both teachers and students. There are various ways and trends for diary writing. Some of them are – *First, a* student's diary may be used as a pedagogic tool. This process provides space to learners to keep their daily diary. These diaries provide a good account of the students' version of classroom practice. The teacher should read those diaries and try to understand the students' perceptions about the class, which can help them to resolve many issues. But what is important here is that the teacher should not be biased after reading these diaries. *Second,* the student's diary may be used to know the different learning styles and accordingly strategies can be developed to teach. These diaries also serve the purpose for various researches as data, not only for the teacher who engaged with it, but others too. *Third,* teachers' diary writing may be used to train teachers exclusively for their CPD. This use of diary writing provides space to teachers for reflection on their own practices which helps them to develop themselves. They accept this learning as they are the constructor of this knowledge.

It is a fact that there are very few diary writing accounts accessible in India. Most teachers do not keep a record and those who do, hesitate to share. In such a situation, it becomes very difficult to understand the notion of diary writing at the application level. It is really appreciable that a few teachers agreed to become part of the present work, by choice.

It is crucial to know that diary writing may include observation, feeling, interpretation, reflection, incidents and so on, separately or all together. Such accounts facilitate the process of understanding the learners' understanding, working and learning. It helps to take better decision about learners' capabilities, regarding what they can or cannot do.

> *"I always keep my eyes on learners, not for what they are doing, but to know what more they can do. I tried to interpret my observations with reflective processes for the implication of learners' learning and my own professional development. I really do not think about the kind of theories, I have read. I just see what exists in practice and try to understand it, with reference to my realistic capabilities."*
>
> *From a teacher's diary*

The above experience of a teacher given in the box conveys that if diary writing is done regularly it may provide a comprehensive base to analyse classroom practices. Maintaining a diary systematically and regularly helps teachers to grow professionally. It is important to know and acknowledge that this development is not sudden and does not provide hands-on solutions, rather, it develops a platform for critical self-evaluation which ultimately helps learners in their progress, not only in terms of the marks/grade they obtained but also as active learners.

It is important to notice that only writing a diary will not serve the purpose, unless we learn to analyse it. It has to be understood that diary writing should become a daily routine, instead of a weekly or monthly routine. It should be written intuitively and not be forced. If teachers feel burdened in writing a diary, it may not benefit them, because it will become a formality to be completed.

> *"I know it is tough to engage oneself with work which you cannot miss. But, I tried a lot for this and once I got familiar with it, it became part of my daily life. And now, it is so obvious to me, that I do it as I take a cup of tea everyday. I am also surprised, about the change I realized within me in a very few days. I strongly believe that if diary writing becomes a part of the teaching community, it will be highly beneficial for learners, as well as teachers."*
>
> *From a teacher's diary*

The above lines in the box show how teachers (who were engaged in the present work) perceive diary writing. The analysis of the diary must be thoughtful and reflective. Teachers should not expect an immediate solution, rather analysis should be done for the development of a perspective. There is no fixed way of looking and analysing these diaries. But a gradual reading of these diaries will help the teacher to revisit and understand the situation and take necessary action. Teachers mentioned that after some time they broadened their outlook. They do not just reflect on these diaries for their own teaching but also, for general teaching. In other words, they learn to theorise the analysis of their diaries.

While doing diary analysis, one has to read and re-read these diaries, as one reading will not provide deep understanding. Each time we read a diary, we engage with a new kind of dialogue, which gives a different perspective. It helps teachers to revisit their earlier classes and understanding about learner, learning and knowledge. It helps them to reconstruct and redesign their pedagogic processes which are beneficial for both teachers and learners. Learners will be benefited because they get improved and better situations for learning and the teacher is benefitted in their self-growth or CPD.

> *"It is true, that whenever I visited my diary, I surprisingly saw something new, and I was amazed to know that, I had missed many things in my earlier reading of my diary. It gives you confidence to read it again, after many readings."*
>
> *From a teacher's diary*

> *"When I revisit my diary, I realize that where I was wrong and what could have been done instead of what has been done. So, it really helps and gives you strength if you re-read your work."*
>
> *From a teacher's diary*

The examples given in the two boxes above are associated with personal actions and insights. There are incidents where the teacher's feelings about learners' behaviour is being reflected. A teacher said, *"I tried a lot, but X really does not want to learn. What should I do?" "I tried my best today, but, if learners are not ready to study what should I do? I felt very helpless today as the class was very unsettled."* The diary clearly highlights time concerns. Time concern here means engagement with diary writing and observing change over a period of time. 'How do teachers upgrade their academic potentialities?' 'What difference do they observe in their own personality?' 'What kind of changes do they perceive in their thinking process etc.?' are very important questions which can be discussed with reference to time frame and change.

> *"I realized that time teaches you a lots of things and this I have learnt. I always give a little gap to reading the diary. And whenever, I read it, I come to know a different perspective."*
>
> *From a teacher's diary*

The examples given in the boxes below share teachers' experiences on the time frame and the change they felt after sharing their diary writing. Some of the teachers said the students' behaviour had also improved, which was a good achievement.

> *"Over a period of time, I grew a lot. I can make a clear distinction to what I was earlier and what am I now."*
>
> *From a teacher's diary*

> *"Today, I learnt that sufficient time must be given to learners so that learning become important, rather, speedup process. I realized, little extra time has given good motivation to the learners."*
>
> *From a teacher's diary*

The teacher understands that over a period of time, it is very important to raise questions to one's own practices and teaching styles, instead of simply giving all responsibility to the learners. Read the given excerpts below from a teacher's diary:

"I am completely surprised at the way I changed my teaching style. It changed automatically, what I generally did in class, now a days it is completely different from my past practices. I am realizing that I developed a lot in terms of language, and I see it as an additional help for learners, because social science is seen as a subject which only deals with concepts, not with language. But I learnt that language plays an important role across disciplines."

"Why does 'X' talk too much in class. Am I failing to reach out to him? Or do I need to change my style of teaching? But which style should I use?

"Why was there no response from the learners' side to my questions? Does it mean, that when I taught them, they did not get it or got something else? Was I little fast today? I think, I should not take up too many issues in a single class."

"I think, I should not scold 'Y'. She was not with me in the class, may be the class was boring? But, what else can I do to get their attention?"

These simple lines of teachers' diaries show how they understand the class and raise many questions of their own teaching styles to think about possible changes.

Another important concern shared by teachers was the concept of groups. A group here means facilitating teaching in groups, where students can work in collaboration. Collaborative work ethos always facilitates learning where each individual not only works collectively but also maintains the importance and space of individuality. Excerpts from the teachers' diaries, given in the boxes below, proves that learners' attitudes towards learning and peer group formation have changed for the positive. They started to enjoy group and collaborative tasks.

"Today, I learnt that sufficient time must be given to learners so that learning becomes important, rather, speedup process. I realized little extra time has given learners good motivation."

From a teacher's diary

"Group work always helps. When I felt students will not be able to do any task alone, I preferred to allow them to do it in groups."

From a teacher's diary

> *"I found a huge change in the learners' ability to learn and think about situations and concerns. In fact, the process of perceiving things has changed in the learners positively."*
>
> *From a teacher's diary*

> *"I would like to highlight their attitudinal changes, rather, learning. They have shown a very co-operative change in their personality, which is really appreciable."*
>
> *From a teacher's diary*

Teachers have reflected on the methodology, as well. This reflection, though very surprising, is crucial. They have a different workload in school, yet they manage to use these innovative methods, which is really appreciable. *"I realize that I should not have used a work sheet for the topic I taught today. It did not work today." "It was good to use the activity in class, students learn better through it but it took too much of time. I have to think something about time management."*

Methodological reflections are very important for a teacher and it has to be internalised, at least at the level of writing. Gradually, this ongoing process facilitates them to develop their reflective thinking for action. Some of the teachers particularly wrote about the timing and space in the classes. *"There is lot to do but how to manage time is a problem with me. Lots of work other than teaching, is always pending. But I have to find out a way."*

In this regard, teachers have written about their own role in teaching. *"I learnt how to improve myself and move beyond the old system to the new system. But I also realized that sometimes the old system is also very important. But, where and how, I have to make a balance, I have to think about it."*

"I took enough time to know that students are more comfortable with me when I am not teaching them officially. Can't I make use of this knowledge? I will try to engage them in a general discussion about teaching."

Teachers confessed that daily diary writing provided them mental strength, as they become capable of thinking and working reflectively. They mentioned they felt very confident about their academic development.

An important aspect that needs to be highlighted here is the style of diary writing. Most of the teachers' diaries show that they had gradually moved to write about the activities they had in class with a reflective perspective in the teaching-learning-process. The two examples given below, from a teacher's diary show this clear difference.

Example 1: *"I did a good job in class today, I used group discussion in class, which worked very well. I am very happy."*

Example 2: *"I tried my level best to deal with the class. The class was fine, yet I am not happy. I think something better could have been done. I have to think about it."*

Gradually, their diary writing process moved from others to themselves. They started writing with reference to others such as like *"they did not listen to me", "how can they learn more", "why were students very casual in the class today"* and so on. Till this point they had the audience in front of them, while writing their diary. But slowly, their focus point of writing the diary moved from others to the self, such as, *"I need some improvement", "how I think about secularism and why"* and so on. This shift helped to reflect upon their own practices.

The diary writing style has a great influence on one's thinking process. Once we start writing something and do it regularly, we see a big difference from where we had begun and where are we now. This difference does not only represent improvement in writing but improvement in thinking also. The dialogue held with the teacher at the beginning of this work, and later showed quite a significant difference. This includes an improved understanding of the teachers towards their students and their learning processes.

Collectively, sharing with others was clearly observed in the later stages of the work. In the beginning, teachers were apprehensive that this process would not feasible, as they won't be comfortable in writing a diary every day, being busy in other assignments. But, very soon, they started enjoying it and this enjoyment put them on the reflective path and therefore on continuous professional development.

Finally, it is important to understand that diary writing is an instrument that gives an inside perspective for professional development and for this purpose, diary writing has great value. It is also important to accept the need to move towards sharing our diary with our colleagues, so that this becomes a general practice wherein a spirit of collective professional development can take place. We need to understand that more professional development can take place with the process of sharing. In other words, it means we need to incorporate diary study with diary writing in the process of continuous professional development.

Here, it is important to acknowledge that diary writing alone will not solve the purpose. We have to use other ways of CPD, as per our need and what we would like to investigate. Yet, diary writing is significant and can be an important and inherent part of all the processes of CPD.

CHAPTER 10

Continuous Professional Development Through Teachers' Research

This work has been done to examine the teacher's role as researcher and enquiry about their professional development. The context of the work has been developed through teachers in Delhi schools, teachers' Continuous Professional Development (CPD), which is important, has emerged out of their school experiences where they value research, a research mindset and enquiry in their own CPD.

The teacher, as a researcher, perceives educational research as a systemic enquiry and it helps them to reflect and improve or strengthen their professional development. It is essential that the teacher's role needs to be explored in the curriculum and research. They must participate in this but the situation is not very satisfactory. One or two teachers in a school are not just enough, the majority of them has to work towards this vision. In other words, the teachers' professional self–image and work conditions require changes.

In the light of this, the present chapter has been written to explore and examine the role of teachers' research and enquiry in their continuous professional development. The base and context of the present study is the interaction and experiences of school-teachers. Here, the attempt is not to evaluate the teachers' conditions, whether they improved or not over the past few years but to understand whether the current development is encouraging and supporting teachers to engage in research and enquiry for their professional development and how the ideas of different theories and models can be seen and applied to CPD in Delhi schools.

A great deal of work has been initiated regarding the research concepts and enquiry and teachers' professional development for the new framework of professional development for teachers. There is a need to describe the knowledge, attributes, values and professional action associated with teaching which can be related to the common standards of

CPD. The teacher as a researcher and active professional should develop the capacity to ensure that teaching is facilitated by research and enquiry, such as:

- Conducting action research and applying the findings.
- Critical reflection on research findings and altering and changing practice is needed.
- Evaluating the gaps and applicability of theory and practice.
- Taking such evaluation further for the betterment of education from policy to practice.

What came out clearly from the discussion with teachers was that they had a tendency to be the sample and consumer (who has already done research), rather than being an active researcher. In the project, we encouraged teachers to be more active in conducting research, in order that they could use their own research findings in their own context and critically evaluate their own work with the help of different research tools and methods.

It is imperative that these practices should and must go beyond the school boundaries. A network should be developed, where inter-institutional practices can be initiated for the teachers' CPD. This will help them to support each other and develop strength towards understanding the teaching-learning process.

An obvious question to ask is whether these expectations are reasonable or not, because earlier and to date, such practices of the teacher as a researcher for CPD has attracted very few teachers, as it is not part of the school system. Only very few self-motivated teachers are associated with this. This chapter aims to understand the above concerns by exploring appropriate theoretical perspectives and by associating these to those teachers' experiences, who participated in the present study. It will be more systematic and useful to talk about a conceptual framework, which would help us to arrive at the different models of CPD and the teacher as a researcher.

CPD of Teachers

CPD can be understood on the basis of different purposes which depends upon the conceptions of teachers' professionalism. The teachers' professional development process should be a self-motivated process, where each teacher has the desire to be professionally developed, leading them towards their individual and collective growth. On the other hand, unfortunately in Delhi schools this process is oriented and governed only by accountability and performance where schools and teachers expect immediate reforms and outcomes of the teaching-learning process, rather than taking it as a tool for professional self-enhancement and development. A distinction can be made between a formal and non-formal mode. The formal approach involves individual engagement with structured programmes provided by an external body. The non-formal approach is characterised by collaborative, mutual engagement in what Wenger (1998) describes as 'communities of practice'. Social interaction becomes important here. It can also be understood as involved participation, mutual engagement and understanding, having a perspective together. For sure, these ideas can be effectively used by teachers to have or conduct research for their professional learning and development.

It is important to highlight that the focus of ways, methods and researches for professional development have changed over the last three decades. This change has occurred because of the changing or evolving meaning and nature of CPD. The earlier understanding about CPD was drawn from the existing theoretical knowledge, but in recent years, experience has become more dominant, where such theories are more respected through those emerged experiences. It was a huge challenge for professional development to have or develop an understanding between theory and practice. This challenge leads to better knowledge and understanding between what kind of theoretical knowledge exists as a higher professional standard, and what actually works and develops in the context and situation. This understanding motivates developing a discourse where teachers subjectively question their own understanding and knowledge by writing about researches they conduct in school for CPD. It involves the teacher as an active participant, where s/he identifies the field of investigation and the method of that investigation.

Understanding Teachers' Research and Enquiry

The study focuses to understand how the use and conduct of research by teachers has strongly influenced by policy; frequent references to teaching; aspiring to be an evidence-based profession; suggests an important and close link between research and classroom practice. But it is not clear whether teachers should use research knowledge which already exists or should teachers be active researchers themselves. Though both need to be used to develop a better understanding about CPD, a lot still needs to be done to realise the better practice for professional development. This combined approach (theory + context) is important, irrespective of any method, tools and techniques. Moreover, there is a need for teachers to be aware of effective research, whether they have conducted any research or not. Teachers should develop abilities to critically and reflectively revisit their own practice and understanding about what they feel is right as a profession regarding their contribution, towards teaching as a profession.

The researches done by teachers can be seen as a systematic and deliberate enquiry about teaching, learning and the entire schooling. Teachers must include empirical, as well as theoretical inquiry, while doing research about any aspect, but they must be aware and critical about the influence of theoretical framework without being influenced, they need to conduct their research to generate new and contextually useful knowledge about CPD. In this way, their research will provide a base to facilitate research happening in the wider spectrum of the teaching community and teacher education. For this, it is important that we consider classroom as an active and live laboratory and teachers as communities of scientists. Here, it is important to mention that the scientific method is not completely appropriate. Specifically, where reflection is involved a subjective approach needs to be used objectively, because there is no ultimate way of reflection and research, it is ever-evolving process. Thus, more dominant constructivist epistemology, rather than positivist conception of truth is better. We need to realise that teaching and learning is beyond simple knowledge and recall. It is important to consider teaching as a public performance which can be scrutinised, shared and discussed with colleagues. Thus, the perception of teaching, as an art, is not a new idea and is being used widely, because teaching not only deals with knowledge and passive elements, but also involves active engagement with learners and their development which is not merely confined to knowledge.

Collaboration, in professional practices and teacher's research, is a highly popular area in literature. But in the Indian research field, this collaborative method of research at the school level is not that prominently visible and reflected upon, especially research in educational settings. Collaborative research can provide a better solution for issues and challenges of practice in the teaching profession. It happens because multiple perspectives exist together and facilitate the work effectively, which could develop a culture of working together or sharing understanding about one's teaching with others to plan and develop with better creativity and productivity.

Teacher research will be able to contribute, whereas actually the collaborative research method is in practice. This collaboration leads to a better understanding about methods such as problem solving, to resolve issues in the long term, which will develop an attitude beyond failure and success in teacher. This will be more effective if it can go beyond the boundaries of a single school and incorporates different schools like a web to develop networking for the school system for CPD which will be more comprehensive and sustainable.

The teacher, as a researcher, will be a better option, rather than the university prescribing something for school education. But it does not mean that school education should not have any relationship with the university (teacher education). Their collaboration will surely develop a more comprehensive discourse of CPD.

In the present study, different aims and objectives have come up for the teacher as a researcher, which includes practice improvement, development, understanding towards professionalism and professional development, practice within and outside the classroom and so on. It is important to acknowledge the existence of the teacher, as a researcher, for positive development in the profession, knowledge and discourse, where the teacher as a researcher and his/her research, must be flexible for critical review by them and others. This again indicates that professional research or development is a collaborative effort, rather than individual effort. Here it is crucial to highlight that teachers' research should not be taken as a separate form of research from the other educational researches taking place in Social Sciences. Doing this will limit the scope of both teachers' research and other educational researches which can help teachers to strengthen their professional decisions. Does the works or practices taking place in school involve a collaborative approach to research? This question can only be answered in the actual realities and practices in the classroom. There are many expectations from teachers, in addition to other responsibilities that they have in school, which will make it tough to engage them in research. But it is true that without any doubt the teacher, as a researcher, will enhance opportunities for professional development because school is considered as a community and not only an individual identity.

Creating Context

It is a universally accepted notion that context plays a significant role in all kinds of practices, whether we are developing or implementing any programme. The same is significant with reference to CPD. Contextual conditions have changed understanding towards CPD, across the world. Research and reflection have been accepted as an effective way or method for professional development. In India, different government as well as private agencies are working towards methods as ways of professional development. At the government level, SCERT is officially responsible for the teachers' professional development but the outcomes are not satisfactory. An analysis of the teachers' interviews shows that the SCERT programmes are merely waste of time and resources. These programmes do not talk about CPD, rather they just provide information that teachers already have. Consequently, the contributions of these programmes are subject to enquiry.

The teacher, as a researcher, has strength for CPD, but teachers reported lack of time as a major obstacle to their actual engagement in classroom action research, although they are very much convinced with the idea. This problem can be addressed by providing the cost of staff cover to release a teacher-researcher from classroom duty to engage in research. However, this will provide a different model of teachers' research where research is embedded in classroom practices.

The basic idea behind this study is to motivate the teaching environment, where development of theory of CPD and practice go hand in hand where practice generates theory and theory facilitates practice. The teacher, as a researcher, contributes extensively to the discourse of CPD because it is derived by means of a thorough and well-grounded empirical process (Christie, 2003).

Two rounds of focus interviews of twenty teachers and other stakeholders, such as parents, students and school officials were done carefully, and an in-depth analysis is done to develop an understanding from the above-mentioned resources. We arrive at certain components for CPD, i.e. personal, professional values and commitment; professional knowledge-based understanding, professional and personal attributes and finally, the profession in action/practice. It is important to mention here that all these components are associated with each other, such as knowledge without practice is meaningless and practice without appropriate knowledge is ambiguous. In the same way, one's knowledge and action without self-criticism will not serve any purpose.

These components and their interrelatedness indicate that the objectives of CPD are not externally imposed by any organisation, rather it is the teachers' owned processes. This process involves professional ethics and professional commitments and that the teacher must situate their knowledge and understanding in the process of reflection and self-criticism. It is important to keep in mind that in this process the teacher is not working only as a technician but should be committed for developing the system and improving professional capacities too. This will lead them towards developing a more reflective method of learning.

Teachers' Experiences and CPD

The study was conducted on the basis of some themes such as: *to learn how to think; to learn how to understand; to learn how to learn and how one thinks* and *to learn in the social context.* The outcome of the study shows the teachers' depth and analytical understanding about research along with critically evaluating their own practice and process of evaluating.

Data from twenty teachers was collected with the help of in-depth interviews and group discussions. They were to observe each other's classes, had to do discussion after classes, write reflective journals and share these with other colleagues. This was part of the project.

The analysis of the practices of teachers with reference to reflection is done on the basis of questionnaire, focus group discussion and review of the given readings. This process of analysis involves different facts on the impact of the reflection, such as critical self-reporting, involvement of new methods and approaches, critical analysis of given articles by researchers and their contribution in general discussions.

The findings were very positive and analytical. It was observed that teachers perceived it as a encouraging, stimulated, critical and reflective process, which helped them in their own teaching practices and experiences, not only related to practice but helped to change their attitude and understanding towards the teaching-learning process.

Some of the teachers appreciated the entire process, by showing renewed enthusiasm and confidence. They said that over a period of time they had lost interest in teaching and became passive as far as teaching-learning and the learners were concerned. But engagement in the project gave them a new space and opportunity to revisit their own practices as a teacher and active practitioner. The boxes given below show the teachers' responses towards the engagement and interest in the project. Teachers found a new way to see the relationship between theory and practice. They accepted that they noticed an improvement in their teaching pedagogy.

"My feeling, to be a reflective practitioner, had been lost somewhere in the past few years. I become very passive in classes because of the school environment and general attitude of teachers towards learning. This initiation has given me a good opportunity to reflect upon my practices and understanding critically."

"This opportunity provided me a chance to evaluate my ways of thinking and understanding. It also helped me to understand the gaps and possibilities, between, theory and practice and this has given a positive and significant shift in my teaching learning process and understanding of how children learn."

A significant change has been reported by teachers in their methods of working. A healthy collaborative environment was developed within the school, where teachers, congenially, shared their practices with each other. They accepted that their method of working has improved. The excerpts given below in the boxes convey that collaborative efforts have changed the teachers' way of reflecting upon their own practices.

> *"A few teachers regularly met after school and discussed each other's professional practices. Though, some were reluctant initially but, gradually this resistance disappeared, and they started collaborative discussion for sharing their learned practices. This has happened because we documented our discussion extensively and kept reading them whenever we got time and we felt like reading it. This process is superb, as far as the professional growth of teachers is concerned."*

Readings provided for their understanding regarding reflection and reflective practices have been appreciated by teachers. Readings strengthened their understanding and developed a context to engage them in this process. They reported, *"the given readings helped to develop a link between the new and existing scenario. We never thought the way we are thinking now about classroom practices and about CPD."* They mentioned that there was hardly any need for refresher courses conducted by SCERT and others, if all schools and all teachers become researchers.

Some of them did raise issues regarding sustainability of this process. They said, *"now we are part of your project, so the school is allowing us to devote this much time to this practice, otherwise, the school may not allow us to do this."*

But what has been very explicitly shown from the analysis (focus group discussions, questionnaires and readings) is that teachers are quite satisfied and happy with the process and wanted to be part of it forever for their CPD as researchers.

Discussion and Conclusion

Achieving the Objective of Educational Research

This study started with the notion that an educational researcher and particularly research conducted by teachers, develops a reflective attitude in them to strengthen the professional development. Teachers show this view very confidently and appreciate the notion of 'teacher as a researcher'. There is a great deal of evidence to prove the strengthened professional decision-making in teachers, such as *"being a teacher researcher,*

I become more confident to use my past experiences in a comprehensive way". "I can take better decisions regarding classroom processes and methods to be used in class". "Reflective processes and process of becoming teacher researcher developed a research aptitude in me which really helps me not only in teaching-learning-processes, but otherwise also." "I feel and realize that, I have become more reflective towards education and its concerns."

These statements prove that the teacher as a researcher helps them in strengthening their CPD, though issues such as lack of time, limited scope, principal's pressure, the given curriculum and syllabus and teaching plans still need to be addressed effectively. There is need to create space for individual autonomy of teachers, support from the school management for research and its better implementation.

Reflective Practices, Teacher as Researcher and Objectives of CPD

One of the basic ideas of the study was to gauge the effectiveness of reflective practices and the teacher, as a researcher, for their CPD. The findings and available facts in the form of teachers' written and verbal responses show that this process has provided them space and opportunities to reflect critically on different perspectives about CPD and the teaching-learning processes. Teachers appreciated the process of exchanging their learning and experiences with other colleagues, which provided them space for better professional development. The combination and interplay between reflective readings, discussions and sharing experiences and taking it critically and reflectively, provided spaces for professional learning. The best part is that they critically perceived and internalised each other's experiences such as *"we discuss about our experiences and learn also but not blindly. I critically evaluate and reflect upon these experiences as per my situation and need."* Thus, evidence shows that this process can be used for CPD and the best part is that it will function from within the school itself.

Research Engagement and Development

The reflective process motivates teachers to be more active in conducting research, apply the research in their own context and critically review their own practices and thinking. Teachers evaluate their experiences and ways of dealing with classes, which shows that their involvement or engagement in this process has provided them an opportunity to become more research minded. It is important to accept that the long-term effect of this process is subject to evaluation. Along with this, how it will help

CPD in the long run in the existing scenario is subject to review and analysis, but this can be evaluated only after these processes get established in the school system.

Some of the researches show a deep understanding about theory and practice. They have shown evidences of developing the ability to theorise from the field.

Collaborative Research Communities

There is a need for the establishment for a community of researching teachers, which needs appropriate infrastructure to facilitate quality research to create space for professional learning and CPD.

It is proved that a collaborative group of researching teachers has the capability to sustain itself. It happens because people in groups working, sharing, and developing expand their vision through each other's ideas and knowledge. They work like communities of practice. Teachers reported that not only they develop knowledge and understanding, but also a shared language on the basis of these small collaborative researches. But there is need to streamline the entire system with a strong political will.

What the Teachers have Gained

It is important for a teacher to know about new innovations taking place in the education field and for that they need to be more equipped with research tools and above all, a research aptitude. It is important because they can critically situate and evaluate their own practices and knowledge, with reference to the changing time and needs and can develop a well-informed point of view.

Evidence that came up from the teachers' views is that they had become more educated in research which shows a clear increase of research literacy. They showed evidence of reflecting on a systematic and organised approach in conducting research. Their evaluative and reflective comments indicate that they are more confident in conducting research and reflecting on the teaching-learning process. They accepted that they have developed a way of generating knowledge with small research studies and that is how they have become more knowledgeable.

To conclude 'teacher research' is a strong tool for professional development. Teachers become more confident and learned to engage themselves in the CPD process they develop and feel ownership of this development which is the study's best outcome.

CHAPTER 11
Metacognition and Reflective Practices

It is important to understand how successful teachers have understood the idea of teaching and professional development. A project was taken up to understand the relation between reflection and metacognition. This includes the documentation of analysis of the processes of reflective processes of various teachers. As a result, meta-cognitive model has been developed for reflection. This also provides space and knowledge about how to improve teaching. This work is a good contribution in the field of reflective practices for improving professional development of teachers.

Theoretical Framework

Why do we need to do reflection? It is a question which needs to be answered. Increased value given to education in last decade has made it more crucial. The demand from a teacher has also been increased. They have to do many works simultaneously, but two important things which they have to do and should do for their own development are *teaching* and *school-based research.* Therefore, they are teachers and researchers as well. Over a period of time a huge shift has been overserved in professional development of teachers. New and various ways have been evolved by various people working in this field and reflection has been used as a metacognitive process. The idea of reflection has been used as a frame of reference. Largely, the ideas of Dewey, Schon, Ramsden etc. have been used as base work, which provides a good strength to the work, as they emphasise the importance to reflection in one way or other.

Reflection is defined as engagement of a person with one's practice which helps him to see old situation in new perspective. But it is also important to mention that neither simple observation nor mindless following of any practice is called reflection. The countless literature is available in the field of reflection but field-based research is not the case, and therefore, most of the available works are theory-based which try to conceptualise the idea of reflection and reflective practices.

This work deals with both the aspects; *first*, it engages with existing theories to enhance theoretical perspective and *second*, it provides strength to the work relating it to the field and grounded perspective; a field-based strength not only to read literature rather grounded perspective is used for analysing to develop a new frame of reflection and reflective activities. While doing this, initially, theoretical construct is used to identify the prevailed reflective processes and then independent construct are identified or constructed. Beginning with these theoretical contexts, actual revelations of school teachers is used to elaborate the major idea of this work which involves reflection – a metacognitive process, thinking about one's teaching and establishing relation with the actual teaching and other associated processes and aspects of teaching which help to make required adaptation with the environment. Therefore, the main objective here is to explain and elaborate upon the models in the study.

Understanding Model

Goals, knowledge, action, monitoring, decision-making and *tolerance* are the important constituents of the model being used here. This model is able to help or facilitate the teacher to work on both dimensions simultaneously, i.e. thought and action. It also provides spaces to develop relationship between present and past, and what can be done in future. Used model provides a multilevel explanatory perspective to teachers, which is not predictive in nature. Now we can understand each dimension separately.

Knowledge and Action

Knowledge and action are two significant components of reflection. Here, knowledge means the detailed and in-depth cognitive schemes which are the result of experience and learning. Whereas action means the outside situation or condition or context where plans and goals are executed and implemented.

Here, it is important to discuss knowledge at little length. Shulman talks about seven such kinds of knowledge in which four are more related to nature of teachers' knowledge. These are *content knowledge, general pedagogical knowledge, pedagogical content knowledge* and *learner's knowledge*. The content knowledge here means subject knowledge; general pedagogical knowledge represents the general ways and techniques for dealing with the class; pedagogical content knowledge talks about the understanding of specific pedagogical knowledge with reference to specific content and area to be discussed and finally, the learner's knowledge here means the kinds of knowledge learners bring to the school as per their age social context and experiences.

Another important aspect related to knowledge is the origin of knowledge teachers' have. It also deals with the epistemology. This entire idea largely talked about two major dimensions of knowledge. First, developing professional knowledge with the help of experience and second, about the different kinds of knowledge which is there but not explicit.

Appropriate knowledge, learning of subject and teaching provide a large perspective about a framework of reflection, which includes the future action, various mechanisms and so on. And this helps in meeting or achieving the goals and objectives.

Goals

Goal can be understood with reference to two aspects. *One* is cognitive which talks about the innate human tendency to work towards goal directed action. And *second* is related to instructional psychology which explains the goal as directive aspect. Therefore, goal is the central point of interaction between knowledge and action. We can also say that the goal may remain constant and process of reflection revolves around it. It is important to mention here that goal remains constant but timely feedback may change it to some extent.

Monitoring and Decision-Making

Here, we are using monitoring and decision-making to develop a way to create linkages between knowledge and action which is directed towards decided goals. The information between teachers and students as external aspect is compared with internal plans which develop the knowledge.

What makes knowledge transferable from one situation to another which influences action, is an important question and answer is decision-making. It is knowledge which provides different ways to analyse the action taken place with reference to the goal. Decision-making also monitors the achievement of the objectives and goals.

Corridor of Tolerance

It is important for a teacher to be tolerant. It is because we do not know what kind of situation one may face during the process of reflection. At times it happens, what has happened is completely contrary to our expectation. Or students may not accept your decision. Therefore, teachers must have patience and tolerance. Tolerance is also important because they have to assess their own teaching, because we may find huge difference between theories we live with and practice we actually adopt in the field. This tolerance does not have any fixed level, it may be needed very little and sometime very high. One's tolerance also depends upon the teaching experience, social context of school, classroom dynamics, familiarity with emerging teaching-learning strategies and so on.

It is also important to understand that these six components may be used innovatively by different teachers to achieve different goals. Therefore, reflection can be understood with reference to:

1) The goals, which use a special plan which is developed on the basis of knowledge,
2) Taking action which can be revised based on feedback, and
3) Feedback is taken care of by tolerance than decision helps take further actions.

Time of Reflection

When reflection will take place (time) is a very tricky question to ask and even to answer. Reflection is a process in which one may live all the time whether 'before teaching', 'while teaching' or 'after teaching'. One may do reflection while interacting and change the way of interaction with others, it is known as reflection-in-action. Sometime reflection may happen after the class, where it would be disconnected to the action but surely benefit the action in future. This also helps to know and analyse the class already taken place, by reflecting whatsoever has happened in the class, to what extent it was successful and so on. Reflection may also occur for future action where one can plan what is expected to do to organise better teaching-learning processes.

Domains of Reflection

It is important to highlight the very idea of reflection with reference to individual differences, which conveys the idea of one's own sphere of reflection where a teacher may feel free to talk to oneself. It is also a fact that various schemes have been given and discussed by various people but what a person actually does has a very different meaning all together. Here, their own interpretation about the theory and action work simultaneously and their varying life experiences may lead them towards varying reflective processes. This varying sphere provides different ways of reflection such as reflection about the epistemology of teaching and learning would be different from the reflection about the success of used teaching method. In this regard, generally we can talk about three kinds of domains:

- *Practical domain*: deals to improve action in a specific situation.
- *Strategic domain*: common or general approaches and strategies for teaching which may be used across the contexts.
- *Epistemological domain*: it deals with the cognitive and metacognitive awareness about one's reflective process.

It is also important to say that though all three kinds of spheres were shown by participants but majority of them used the practical sphere for their reflective processes.

Reflection — a Meaning

As stated above, the process of developing present model (suggested by author) includes the theoretical understanding first and then actual practice of school-teacher. These two combined processes provide a detailed understanding of how reflection is represented in actual action. Therefore, the meaning of reflection here is a process of thinking at cognitive and meta-cognitive levels about the teaching-learning processes and practices with the help of monitoring which include the passage of tolerance and making appropriate decision to achieve the goal of better teaching-learning processes and practices. Here, the process of monitoring and decision-making along with goals is the main or core of the process of reflection. The monitoring process and decision-making create a bridge between knowledge and action. And this bridge provides better scope for developing better teachers.

Exploration of the Reflective Process of Teachers

Here, a brief description is given about the design of the study which helped to understand the entire work done in the field including verification, exploration of the model, ways of analysis and finally analysis of data.

Method and Data Sources

The presented praxis-based model of refection has been developed on the basis of the engagement we had with school teachers about their reflective practices, where they share their perspective on reflection which was supported by their retrospective experiences. Five humanities teachers from different schools in Delhi, having minimum 10 years of teaching experience at secondary level were the part of this inquiry.

These teachers were selected on the basis of pilot phase where we interacted with them and find out their reflective understanding. All of them have recognition as good teachers in school. Students were also involved in the process and their views about teachers were also kept in mind while choosing these teachers. Another dimension which was kept in mind is who was showing more meta-cognitive abilities during interaction. The idea was to develop a best document about reflective practices based on meta-cognitive abilities.

All the teachers were given same topics of Class IX to teach. It is important to mention that while analysing it was kept in mind that even the class and content were same, but the school context and learners' backgrounds were different. A simple but effective process was used where these teachers were interviewed before the class and after the class. Observations were also done during the teaching. This provided a good data for analysis. We also requested teachers to allow us for video recording of their classes, but they refused to do so, otherwise we could have presented a more comprehensive picture of the reflective processes. Class size, more or less, was same in all the schools.

Coding Scheme: Development and Reliability

Data collected was reviewed time and again. A kind of triangulation was used, where before class discussion, observation and then after class discussions were incorporated. In this triangulated process, initially, focus was more on understanding the monitoring, knowledge and decision-making ability. It was found that these abilities were shown by teachers, but, not in a fixed manner or sequence. We also identified some examples which can be called episode and are used for analysis. These episodes showed clear relationship between monitoring, decision-making and goal attainment. Teachers also explained these episodes for better analysis.

An example of episode: *I tried my best but still not getting the answer which, I feel student should give at this level [monitoring], therefore, I think, I should be letting them go on their pace with discussion [decision]...... I was expecting them to say 'Democracy' [cue that did not emerged], so I told them [decision – way of engagement also changed] because they were not reaching to the correct point [still monitoring].*

The coding process can be understood in four ways, where preceding one is more elaborated.

- Evidence (first way)
- Evidence of the components of reflection (second way)
- More specific coding of above two (third and four)

The *first* way is developed or taken from the literature available about reflection and it incorporates three aspects: *practical, strategic* and *epistemic.* The *second* way deals with the two acts of the present model: *monitoring* and *decision-making* which were taken or developed from literature available on meta-cognition. The *third* way of coding drawn from the combined interpretation of theories and collected data, which deals with monitoring and decision-making in a more elaborated manner. What and how something evaluated was associated with monitoring and what and when something got changed associated with control. Goal was also coded because it was the focus of the entire episode. Finally, the *fourth* way emerged from collected data in more details in compare to third way.

Monitoring: When teachers recall what have they done or gone through in the class. There was certain stimulus on which teacher see the effect of his/her teaching or action in class. Some examples are–students writing, space, and verbal communication and so on.

How Evaluated: Teacher evaluated these cues in four ways: optimistic, neutral, pessimistic and mixed (optimistic and pessimistic).

Decision-Making and *What changed:* The kinds of changes can be understood in various categories, such as changes related to teaching strategies, content, instructional material and so on. In each of the episode the kinds of changes were done, the type of change was coded. Time is the main factor during any change in decision-making about any change. This at later stage finally leads towards reflection.

Goal: Two categories of goals were identified, first focuses on teaching and other focuses on learning. Teaching is more managed by teachers because of dealing with teaching methods and content, whereas learning goal is more associated with learners where students' participation and engagement with learning is focused.

Knowledge: It was found that knowledge can be understood in two ways. *First,* explicit (overt) knowledge, which is available in textbooks, using this knowledge across contexts such as knowledge related to pedagogy or content. *Second,* emerging or developing knowledge. Knowledge, which is not generalised and can only be understood and explained with reference to feelings, thoughts and past experiences.

Therefore, an episode can be coded in the context of practical sphere, which is related to first way (evidence). What cues were evaluated would be related to monitoring and how it was evaluated would be associated with third way (more specific way related with the coding way one and two). And finally, learners' writing, time, etc. as well as optimistic, pessimistic and mixed related to fourth way of coding. If we have to change any decision (second way of coding) than these all changes will be coded in third and fourth way, just like with monitoring and knowledge and goal were also coded in a similar way.

Discussion

Teachers' reflections and reflective ways and processes are incorporated in the analysis. Once the coding was over, a small meeting or get-together was organised where the codes and model was presented to them. Their final view to this was observed and recorded. Most of them accepted that they were doing the same thing which has been mentioned, though they have not thought to articulate it. Most of them accepted that they were not aware of what they were doing. It is also important to mention here that towards the end of this meeting they started using the language of the model about the evaluation of their teaching.

The result of the study was presented with reference to who they reflect upon their teaching, which was discussed with reference to the components of the reflective model. What focused here was the improvement in teaching with reflection.

Goals

What has to be achieved represents the meaning of goal here, along with the action to be taken to achieve them. It can be understood, when teachers take decision to make changes in their strategies for better adjustment with the situation and can be seen the achievement of the goal. In reflective episodes, most of the teachers achieved their goals related to methodology, content along with student engagement and participation. Student understanding and learning was also up to the mark.

Except these goals, teachers achieve more objectives than teaching-learning. They achieve the goal which may be indicated with reference to their experiences as school teachers. It also came out from the data that teachers have used different theories which deals with the developmental changes of the learners. Some of them managed to use theoretical understanding of psychological theories to understand about the learner, learning and knowledge.

Monitoring

Monitoring is a process which helps to develop a relationship between expected outcome and real (actual) action to achieve these expected outcomes. It directly deals constantly to achieve the set and emerging goals of the action. Another aspect of monitoring is related to knowledge which provides help and facilitation in evaluation. Also, the knowledge to make correct choice about the facilitation, which is used in terms of clues, cues, etc.

What Evaluated: The very important exploration was most of the teachers attended to and evaluated clues from the learner; the percentage was 79.

How Evaluated: Optimistic, neutral, pessimistic and mixed are taken as evaluation of cues. 40% of the evaluation was neutral, where all monitored their goal regularly, irrespective of situation. 36% of evaluation deals with optimistic aspect, which includes the teachers feeling about the acceptability of the teaching towards achieving the goal. 14% of the evaluation was pessimistic and 10% of the evaluation is mixed.

The Tolerance: This tolerance provides initial explanation, which needs further elaboration. We understand that the optimistic evaluation is more within the individual passage of tolerance and, therefore, less likely to take up change than other evaluation. Passage of tolerance allows the little progress towards goal very optimistically. Cues being monitored that fall outside the passage of tolerance are deemed not acceptable, and the teacher likely makes decisions to modify the teaching.

It is important to note that most of the time the cue or clue comes under the passage of tolerance. Teacher made little changes in the pre-planning. Teacher changed their plan only 30% of the time of their monitoring. As has been thought of, pessimistic evaluation happened more frequently than optimistic or mixed evaluation. This episode which changed was 28% and these were evaluated pessimistically.

14% episodes, which lead changes, were evaluated optimistically and 12% episodes which lead changes had been evaluated mixed. Therefore, it can be said that there were all kinds of evaluation which lead to change, but pessimistic evaluation had more significant role and weightage.

What is more interesting to know here is that the 43% of the episodes that lead to change had been naturally evaluated. But most of such changes were of minor and it was acceptable that these changes were made to improve pedagogical processes by teachers, which provides them opportunities to have optimistic experiences from the monitored cues. This very idea works as re-investment in cognitive sphere, and it happens because one needs to be developed as a teacher, initially with performance issues and later with effective teaching. Thus, teachers were engaged in becoming effective practitioners.

Decisions

Decision is a process which allows knowledge to be used to adapt or change as a result of evaluation. Outcome of the present work shows that change in instruction is due to evaluation.

What Changed: Most of the changes were done in methodological ways and content, where methodological change was noted 40% and content change 40%. These two played a large or an important role in the process of reflection, which was under the control of teachers. Other kinds of changes were about 9%. It is important to note that the change of methodology and content was directly associated with the learning. It may also be seen as teachers' own interest of improving their abilities as a teacher. It is important to understand if one will be able to resolve the performance issues initially in career, then later may be dealt effectively with other learning-related issues of students, such as innovative methods and their relations with learning processes.

It is important and largely acceptable that objectives and evaluation are two significant elements of instruction, about changes in objective and evaluation were found very low. (Approximately 1 or 2%). It was found that teachers hardly made any major changes in objectives and evaluation while teaching, rather it was found that they made more changes in objectives and evaluating their content and methodology outside the class.

Here, it is important to highlight that teachers made few changes in their evaluation system. Yet, they were sensitive enough towards students' learning, because lots of informal assessment were the part of their teaching-learning processes.

When Changed: The interest of a person motivates for change. Most of the changes were made to achieve the goal or those were in favour of achieving the goal in a specific class, because teachers managed to make most of the changes on the spot while teaching, which shows the abilities and experiences of teachers. Whatever may be the reason behind these abilities, but it shows teachers' courage and ability to take risk about their own pre-planning. This is also an indicator of the ability of reflection-in-action. This also helps us to identify the important role of knowledge in reflection, which can never take place with a good and strong knowledge base, which always works as a platform to use various pedagogies in class course.

Knowledge: Knowledge provides an important base to plan, monitor and decision-making along with reflection. It was found that whether teachers change their pedagogy or not, but while monitoring and decision-making, pedagogical knowledge played a major role. All the teachers were confident about their knowledge that they were able to elaborate about the rationale for their monitoring and decision-making. These abilities also prove teacher's command over different kinds of knowledge whether it is procedural or factual, such knowledge always develops after experience. Their self-observation: "*I always teach in front of the class*" shows their honest and micro-level analysis of their own action, which also shows the basic characteristics of their teaching.

It is interesting to note that teachers who had some kind of training about any specific topic were less able to draw more from teaching experiences, whereas others were more able to use their teaching experiences in teaching and pedagogical processes. These teachers sometimes were not able to name the knowledge but were able to use it.

This wide range of knowledge provides abilities to develop and create new and innovative plans and also to take right decision at right time to make necessary changes. This kind of flexibility was based on the huge experience teacher had. Along with this, monitoring on results provides space to develop new knowledge or re-development of existing knowledge. It can also be said that knowledge is very significant for reflection and reflection also develops new knowledge, therefore, experienced teachers were able to develop themselves as effective reflective practitioners.

Sphere of Reflection

Strategic reflection deals with the process of generalisation, where we can develop and use some common ways to deal with the situation across the context, whereas epistemic reflection involves awareness or knowledge about one's own way of reflection. Here, it is important to know that epistemic reflection does not provide immediate solution, rather gradually develops ability to use other kinds of abilities. It is also important to know the teachers without prior training, were more able to draw more generalised pattern than teachers who already had training because their thinking and cognitive processes are enculturated in already developed knowledge.

Conclusion

There is no single way or pattern of reflection; rather, there are ways of reflective practices. Academic, social efficiency, developmental, social reconstruction and generic orientation of reflection are few of such ways.

The generic reflection is one which can consider all kinds of reflection is good, because it provides full and free space for reflection and therefore free-thinking processes.

Our work is also more focused on the last kind of reflection, where reflection is based on day-to-day practices in classroom. This has strength to improve daily practices a teacher and students have to go through.

What we analyse is also the day-to-day practices (reflective processes) of five teachers, which also include the instructions (pedagogies) and learners' education. The outcome is a meta-cognitive model of reflection and coding. These provide a way to analyse practices in form of reflection and, therefore, a specific way of thinking and improving one's teaching processes as reflective practitioners.

CHAPTER 12

Professional Development and the Learner-Centered School

Paradigm Shifts in Professional Development

Dharmesh, a teacher in secondary school teaching Social Science, is always motivated to teach and engage with learners. In his seven years of service, he tried all possible methods of teaching and pedagogic processes. Yet he accepts that practically he has not achieved the objective. The reason he points out is that school is not learner centered. Therefore, the very ideas of child-centric education get defeated. He says that the idea of professional development of teacher is mainly associated with learner-centered school system. He registered his helplessness during author's interaction with him. He favours the idea of child-centered education, where focus is more on learners than anything else. Dharmesh visited many schools and conducted a study which indicated that the child-centered schools provide better opportunities for professional development because teacher-student relationships become more intense and closer, which provide them space and opportunities for reflection on one's action. He specifically mentioned that reflection and professional development of teachers are closely related. And suggested that need is more to develop a learning community within and across the school, so that a comprehensive space can be provided for professional development which will be beneficial for both teachers as well as learners.

Above-discussed ideas of a motivated teacher are providing spaces to develop a better professional development opportunity for teachers. Many insights can be drawn from these to understand the teachers' professional development. We now discuss about the traditionally perceived meaning of professional development.

It is important to know that in most of the situations in India teachers' continuous professional development is perceived as a need of teachers. It sounds like everything is depending on the teachers, therefore professional development is the need of the teachers. This very idea has ignored the active participation of other stakeholders such as students, school administration, parents and so on. It has been accepted widely that only teachers' professional development can be catered by dealing with the need of the teachers.

Another important aspect of continuous professional development which prevailed is individual development. Therefore, the idea of professional development is restricted to the development of a teacher. It fails to see the very idea of collective or systemic development. It is essential to argue here that the idea of professional development which focuses only on an individual may not facilitate for longer. The spirit of collectiveness and systemic development is more crucial and important then individual development. One has to consider school as a social community, and community development will lead the development of an individual. Because the idea of individual development is prevailing, therefore, it is believed that new and emerging knowledge skill and pedagogic processes can be transmitted in teachers and transmission can be used to teach learners. The idea seems to prove that teachers are not capable to generate ideas and knowledge whereas students are able to. This dualistic and dichotomic idea revives the very idea of continuous professional development, where teacher has to play an active role. Transmission conveys the understanding of decades old view of behaviourism, where teacher seems to look an empty pitcher and experts fill it and then teachers would deal with learners. This very idea of transmission can also be questioned with reference to contextuality of pedagogic processes. This idea of transmission goes against the idea of context embedded pedagogic processes.

This prevailed idea of professional development consists of the understanding of external intervention, where some external agencies organise professional development programmes from time to time. This works like a training and not as education or learning. The idea of training works on the principle of working on the abilities (ability-based) of teachers with various engagements, but it never sees professional development as an embedded learning process which can completely be understood with reference to job they are doing.

Traditional idea of professional development deals with generic teaching skills. It does not deal or focus on content specific pedagogical skills. Its main purpose is restricted to provide general understanding about teaching-learning processes. It works on the principle of general approach, which can be used in specific situation only and therefore, a general overview about teaching-learning is supported by them. But this idea has weaknesses, because teaching-learning is always specific to content and context, therefore, general teaching ways and strategies may not be useful and effective as expected.

Another important aspect which needs to be discussed here is the kind of engagement one has with reference to professional development. Is it short term fragmented or long term and coherent? If professional development is perceived as a piecemeal and short-term engagement, probably the rate of success will be very low, as teachers will consider it as given task which they have to do. They will do it and then forget it. This kind of short and fragmented intervention does not help the processes of progressive professional development of teachers. Therefore, it is important to accept that yearly short-term engagements will not facilitate the actual process of professional development of teachers.

An important aspect regarding teachers' professional development is who takes major and crucial decision about professional development of teachers. Is it school or some agencies outside of the school? We have to accept the importance of school-based decision-making regarding teachers' professional development. It is also important because school is the best agency, to assess the actual need of the school system. School can understand the two-fold objectives of professional development of teachers i.e. *professional growth of teachers* and *learners' development*, therefore, crucial and significant decision about teachers' professional development should be taken within the school.

We also have to understand that professional development of teachers is not the growth or development of few teachers. Rather we have to understand it as a larger phenomenon which talks about the professional development of all the teachers, where equal opportunities are to be given to all. The idea of collectiveness and community has already been discussed, which provides strength to the process of professional development of teachers. Collegiality, togetherness, cohesiveness and many other such features will be left out if we restrict the idea of continuous professional development with reference to the development of few teachers.

Another important aspect regarding professional development is that it should be essential for all instead of few teachers. Such environment needs to be created where everyone feels the need for their professional development.

This above discussion highlighted various aspects of existing and prevailed practices of CPD in India. In brief, these are:

- Teachers are at the centre.
- Personal development is focused.
- Restricted only to skill and methodologies.
- Short programme which happens once in a year.
- It focuses on decision-making.
- Specific objective based, and
- Teachers' need based.

Understanding Professional Development

The paradigm shift in professional development has an interesting history, where the shift has taken place from teachers-centered to student-centered, few teachers to all, optional to essential and so on. It is a fact that initially development of teachers planning was based on teachers' need. It was not based on the achievement of learners, rather based on teachers' knowledge and skill development. This idea was prevailed that the professional development of all the teachers is not required, rather it is required only for those who have problem in teaching processes. But now the idea has changed and has been established as a requirement of all the teachers for their professional growth/development. It has become more learner-centered than teacher-centered. Therefore, it becomes important to understand these changes in little more elaborated manner.

Based on Learners' Performance

It has been observed widely that the moto of professional development was to engage teachers as per their need and requirement, which had hardly concerned with students' performance. It was not seen as a tool for the development of both teachers as well as learners.

It has been observed that recently teachers' professional development has shifted from very general orientation to the performance of students in a particular work or ability, such as performance in mathematical ability, etc. The focus of inquiry has moved from teachers' performance to learners' performance.

Focus on Systemic Development of Individual

This very idea of collective and systemic professional development takes us to the realm of school as learning community. Earlier focus was more on the development of individual's abilities, skills, knowledge and so on, where prime objective was to develop potential in teachers. This idea looks good but over-emphasis on an individual hinders the process of collective development.

The new idea of systemic development is a better process, where a feel of collectiveness, collegiality and cooperation exists in a relatively stronger manner, instead of focusing only on individual professional development.

Though it is a fact that a teacher will perceive system on the basis of perspective he/she carries. On the other hand, it is also a fact that a systemic socialisation provides them a better space and understanding of professional development.

Action Research in Teaching and Learning

Traditionally experts' role was dominant in professional development of teachers, where teachers' knowledge, experience, etc. were hardly given any importance. Their questions were considered unimportant for inquiry, because university experts suppressed them. Whereas it is required to acknowledge the importance of teachers' experiences and knowledge, as they are the actual practitioners in the field. On the basis of their own experiences, the development process can be initiated, which may lead them to the highest level of professional development. This will help them to take responsibility of their own work, they are engaged with.

Acknowledging their experiences help them to reflect about their own past practices and also help them to monitor the learners' growth. This is a longitudinal process, but effective.

This process acts like a loop, where teachers come with enriched experiences from the field and discuss/share the same with others and then again go back to the school, this process rotates in a cyclic manner. This sharing of experiences enhances teachers' perspective about school, classroom, learner, pedagogy and so on.

Job Oriented Professional Development

The idea of CPD which prevailed was job-oriented, because their job promotion is tied to this, though it provided some kind of professional development to teachers. These kinds of programmes actually take place beyond the school boundaries, which limit its importance and usefulness, because, the relationship between field, challenges and solutions is weak in this model. Therefore, it becomes essential to provide opportunities and spaces for their professional development within the actual field i.e.

school, otherwise the transformation of learning during such courses/programmes will not be transferred to the actual situation. Whereas it is a fact that learning should be transferred horizontally, vertically, bilateral and so on, but to what extent these courses will be able to help teachers is a matter of concern.

Content for Professional Development

It is very significant to understand that what kind of content has been interacted among the teachers. Is this content very general which is applicable to all situations or does it have some specific characteristics? It is observed that general approaches are not much useful for effective teaching. It may only help in engaging learners in class, but what kind of engagement is taking place is also crucial. Therefore, there is a requirement of some specific kinds of engagement. This specific engagement needs to be organised around the specific subject area. It is important and crucial because need is more to understand the nature and epistemology of the content and pedagogical practices used. It is important to acknowledge the above relationship to provide appropriate space to learners for learning. This provides a better scope of continuous professional development of teachers.

Short Term versus Long Term Plans

It is important to understand that the job/assignment one is going to be engaged with is of short term or long term. Initially short term strategic processes are appreciated but later it was realised that long term engagement is more significant as far as professional development is concerned. Long term engagement provides space and opportunities to understand the situation and the problems where follow up is also possible, which is not the case with short term engagement. Doing many short-term engagements, better is to get engaged with long terms programmes, so that a healthy and comprehensive perspective can be developed. Longitudinal engagement provides better and relatively stable solution to the problems. Continuous professional development itself is a gradual and longitudinal process, therefore, the engaging process which equipped us for the purpose of continuous professional development should be longitudinal.

Professional Development is Not Occasional; it is Embedded in Everyday Life

Continuous professional development cannot be conceptualised if it happens occasionally through some specific programmes, such programmes seem to be ritualistic than actually helpful. Therefore, there is a great need to develop continuous professional development process which is part of everyday life of the teachers, and not for the specific occasions. It should have become one of the general responsibilities of teachers, where they do not feel burdened rather accept it as the routine work. When teachers participate in continuous professional development process with full legitimate participation, they grow as better professionals. The very idea of community participation can be used here to make this entire process more useful and meaningful for teachers, where every teacher will have to take part in the community of practices.

Professional Development is the Responsibility of all, not of Few

Earlier the idea of professional development was perceived as a responsibility of few people, whereas need is to make it everybody's responsibility, where each one is responsible for their own work and actions. They have to feel responsibility to develop teaching as a social practice and to achieve this, they have to take part in various activities of their professional development. Everyone's participation will ensure a successful continuous professional development process with reflection. This will also lead us towards professional development of everyone, where the idea of essentiality works over selection or voluntary choice. The essential features surely develop the accountability and responsibility in school practitioners. But we also have to keep in mind that teachers' professional development cannot take place in isolation, it has to be associated with learners' life.

It has to be kept in mind that the kind of discussion taken place above is not very easy to implement. Questions such as what methods and approaches will affect the changes? What factors might influence to success of the continuous professional development? How should we know, what will facilitate the transition from present situation to a more developed situation? Here, we also have to understand that there is no final and sure solution for anything, though; adapting ways with reflective mind can facilitate entire process of continuous professional development. We also have to understand that very evolved idea of continuous professional development is emerging in India but there are some issues and challenges also. But initiation provides hope of possibilities to change the situation.

To take such initiative, there is a need to change the existing Indian school system. Moreover, beyond system, mindset also needs to be changed. This argument has a strong potential that alone neither teachers nor the system are able to make the required change, rather there is a need of collaborative effort from both the sides. This collaboration will lead entire school education towards a better platform, where teachers' objectives and aims may be personal, but will deal with the larger concerns of the entire school system from knowledge, to learning, to learners. Once these systemic changes take place the very progressive vision of continuous professional development will be able to take place. Such system will be self-sustainable where no outside agency intervenes unnecessarily. But it also does not mean that because of systemic hazards, one will just wait to get these hazards to be removed from the system. Somewhere, we have to take a step to begin our continuous professional development. This beginning may include brief staff meetings, teaching teams, action researches, field work during vacations, development of curriculum, developing and maintaining learning groups, etc.

We also have to acknowledge that time constraint is a important hurdle in the pathway of continuous professional development, therefore a teacher has to be creative enough to make best use of the available time.

It is also important to understand that change needs to move from both the sides i.e. top-down and bottom-up. All have to work with the commitment for exploration, consensus building, mutual support and other systematic reforms and collaboration.

Beside these, one also has to think critically and develop a perspective to learn and understand about the required changes and strategies for CPD. Many questions need to be understood at length, such as–How does professional development happen? What are its paradigms? What is the need to study about professional development? What kind of possibilities does it create for professional development? And so on.

Finally, the overall school environment needs to be developed on the basis of progressive education, where each agent (child, teacher, administration, etc.) in school gets actual and required space. School must share some common values such as collaboration, collegiality, experimentation, diversity, democracy, inclusion and so on. These ways will make a radical change in the entire school system and lead towards a healthy and collaborative system among teachers, students, curriculum, pedagogy and evaluation.

CHAPTER 13

Reflective Teaching

It is a reality that when we borrow any system (either political or educational) from any other source, it loses its essence and originality from many points of view, the most important is related to its applicability. The same is true with words, terms and concepts taken from other disciplines. This has happened with the term 'reflection' which is basically associated with philosophy and psychology and now, at a wider level, we are trying to use it in education. It has received a lot of attention, particularly in teaching and developing reflective skills and the ability of reflective teaching based on personal theories, instead of already given or established theories. This helps teachers to critically theorise their practice.

There are basically two forms of reflection. The first accesses the non-logical, procedural knowledge used in ongoing practice. In this case, reflection is in the action and only truly manifested in the phenomenology of the practice itself (Carr, 1987, Schon, 1983). The second deals or talks about the practitioner's own knowledge and ways of doing, acceptance, alteration and changes beyond the current situation.

It is possible to identify a few common characteristics of different types/forms of reflection. These common characteristics may help to overcome the problems and contradictions found in the field of reflection and can create space for progressive change, from the process of knowledge development. Reflection, in this form, will be omnipresent, a continuous or ongoing process, which will not only talk about knowledge practice, but try to develop a link and association between knowledge and society and its concerns. We could keep in mind that associating oneself with a single practice/way of reflection, will limit the scope of reflection in itself. It is very tough to say that these are the only characteristics of reflection and if one learns those, he/she will become a reflective practitioner, because the process of reflection evolves, and it is not something given.

The crucial points or arguments given below are important regarding education and reflection:

1) Reflection is a tool to bridge the gap. It means how do we fill the gap about what is happening and what can happen for one's betterment. In other words, how does transforming happen reflectively from one course of action to another, which can lead us towards development.
2) The above argument about filling the gap and transforming should be seen in professional practices and if not, then there will be a contradiction.
3) Its implementation or use in education limits its scope, particularly in terms of benefits and achievements.

Reflection as a Bridging Process

The use of reflection in education to bridge or fill the gap has three major components: a) deliberate or motive oriented reflection, b) reflection as filling the gaps and c) function of association of perspectives.

Deliberate or motive oriented reflection: Reflection has always been planned and deliberated. One sets out a purpose and then acts to achieve it. We never do reflection by chance or accidentally. As it is deliberately done by a person, it becomes ego driven. Popper and Eccles (1977), Dennett (1979) stated that one has tried to include categories of intentional thinking, such as reflection, wholly within mechanistic explanations. It is important to know that 'meta' as a label or term has been used to talk about thinking, over thinking or thinking about thinking, which represents one's view about his/her own way of thinking. It also makes a person think deliberately and impose self-supervision regarding so-called reflection which includes memorising, recalling, reserving and so on.

It is important to consider that in education ownership of our work is crucial. It means we are responsible for our actions, which develops a sense of responsibility. It has a direct linkage as we think before we do, and thus we are responsible for what we do and when we reflect. It implies that our reflective gains not only help us in a particular situation, but also help to select or reject certain things (scrutiny). Pedagogic decision-making, as reflective practice, has been favoured by Buckmann (1986), Schon (1987), Clarke (1991), because they believe that reflection is governed by ethical considerations.

Therefore, here reflection has been perceived as a self-driven process, which is deliberately done and as such it carries the responsibility of reflective practices.

Reflection as filling the gaps: Reflective abstraction has an important role to play in cognitive development. According to some, it is the tendency of a human being to dissent from a previously existed understanding/perspective to a new one on the basis of experience and develop a new conceptual knowledge/understanding. In other words, in our challenging life we encounter new situations and experiences and their interaction help us to develop a new perspective. If we consider reflective processes are crucial and important, then Vygotskian views seem important regarding the development of reflection in children. This view believes that the process of construction and reconstruction is an ongoing process, which facilitates the reflective process. Moreover, reflection is important not only for cognitive restructuring, but also for composing an internal dialogue with oneself, which enables us to understand one's own practice and thinking, which leads towards self-awareness and, therefore, self-control. Reflective practices here lead to the previous understanding of a constructive change, and this construction and re-construction are highly associated with reflective thinking.

In the reflective process there are essential linkages between old and new perspectives. In this process, some already existing views and understanding is always revisited to discover new possibilities. It means the reshaping/restructuring of a previously existed point of view and, thus, it contributes in the development of new knowledge.

One major importance of reflective practice is that it helps to find associations between two perspectives and this combination creates space to develop a new understanding. It not only reviews the past, but provides guidelines for future action, as well. It is important to realise that perspective is not only a point of view, but realises the content of whatever is scanned for purposes generated by the perspective taker (Mezirow, 1978). In other words, it means looking at one perspective in terms of another. We think about our thinking and try to change it. The success of reflection lies within its process, where it is not merely revisiting past practices, but revisiting it analytically, critically, in a unified manner, thus helping to bring oneself from one state to another. This bridging helps in the transformation from the old to the new, showing that our path has developed by destroying what we have left behind.

Therefore, breaking and repairing give strength to the reflective process and this happens due to a web of perspectives which develop through the association of different perspectives from different viewpoints. The assumption behind this is that the origin, development and function of concepts are context embedded.

Reflective Practitioner

Practitioners, generally, do not use prepared strategies, leading them to take on the spot decisions, which again can create problems because they take random, non-conscious and judgemental decisions for planned and conscious ends which somehow result in the practitioners usual behaviour.

Reflection is a way of converting available structured experience into newly structured action that we call professional practice. Surely, it should work for positive change, as in the absence of such change it will be difficult to see what and how things are missing from the knowledge and understanding that has been acquired. It is important to see how reflection creates a link between thinking with action. Differing with Polayn and Prosch (1975), Schon believed that reflection not only exploits tacit knowledge, integrating it with conscious activity, but progressively redesigns it, with a new perspective. Schon's idea on reflective functions is – as we are not aware of its mechanisms and there is no need to rigidly place it in a step-by-step sequence.

Bridging the Gap from Practice to Theory: The Normative Role of Reflection

Many thinkers are worried about the precision and utility of reflection. They doubt if construction-reconstruction can make reflection normative. An important question that arises here is, 'Is it possible that by helping teachers to improve their strategies, they can become reflective practitioners?'

Whatever value judgement a teacher makes should essentially facilitate or guide better understanding and associated skills, in order to locate different processes for practical purposes. Reflectivity in theory and practice are different, therefore, for a better understanding or implementation of reflective practices, it is essential to have some sort of rationalisation between them and in the absence of this rationality, teaching as a unitary function will remain confused. The teacher's own knowledge has a significant role to play here.

We reflect in different ways, as we experience things and events differently, and therefore our purpose of reflection is also different. On the other hand, reflection is a reviewing process, which occurs within a perspective forcing us to interpret one thing in terms of another, this leads us to transform what has been revisited. It is true that dependency on one skill may distort the entire process of reflection. Initially, teachers may remember small bits of reflection which could help them to initiate or induct in the reflective practices, and slowly the outcome of one act of reflection ought to link the purpose of another. This process has flexibility, potential and capability of gradual progress.

Thus, reflection is a process where practitioners exploit their personal knowledge when they reconstruct knowledge and form different perspectives, including context. This leads to the path of construction – reconstruction – combination and transformation (progressive development).

We can learn from others with the help of reflection. It can be said that this works as a means of knowledge transfer, a means of learning something which may not be completely useful in another situation but has the ability to select (scrutiny) certain things to be used possibly in another context. With regard to this, Stenhouse (1975) sees the importance of the action research model, which is fundamentally based on actual practice.

The normative role of reflection has been perceived by Van Manen (1991) who states that this depends on the motives that generate it. Others take personal and tacit knowledge as a bridge towards more formal theories, but it is true that personal theories are stronger, and it is not so easy to reconcile them with idealistic conceptions. Thus, the facilitation of this idealistic knowledge helps practitioners to move ahead from one level of reflection to another.

Undoubtedly, practitioners could face problems and hazards to move from one level of reflection to another. Unless practitioners see the transforming capacity of reflection, no theory can help them. They will be stuck with different theories and theoretical notions and become part of a process, without any reflective vision.

Reflection as a Primary Educational Process

Limiting reflection to a single formula does not do justice to the concept itself. With this limitation, reflection cannot facilitate the qualitative, cognitive process. Actually, reflective practitioners, according to Schon (1983), are those who can reframe past experiences in a new manner, based on their needs and challenges towards transformation. But, Schon could not give appropriate weightage to bridging the ability of reflective thoughts, whereas Pollared (1989), perceived reflection as a key in rationally devising the teaching-learning process, different from Schon.

As discussed earlier, reflection is a general process, having transformational ability and can help practitioners to gain benefits in professional development with organised knowledge development.

Thus, we can say that reflection is a widely used concept in education and more possibilities are visualised in the teacher's continuous professional development. In recent years, it has been a largely used and discussed model. It has led to the belief that reflective teaching is considered good even without understanding the procedure of reflection, particularly the reasons for reflective action. What a teacher reflects for and about are more significant to their professional development or success than if do not reflect at all.

There is no doubt that reflective practice has merits for continuous professional development. To understand reflective teaching as a transformational bridge between knowledge, society and learners, more work is needed with regard to its educative power and capabilities for professional development. If a teacher community gets reflectively developed, it can contribute to policy making as can be seen in many nations across the world. However, teachers/practitioners have to understand that it is an ongoing and never-ending process, which needs continuous, active commitment towards teaching as a profession.

CHAPTER 14

Mentoring and Continuous Professional Development

Teacher mentoring programmes have dramatically increased since the early 1980s as a vehicle to support and retain novice teachers. The vast majority of what has been written about mentoring has focused on what mentors should believe and do in their work with novice teachers. The professional literature, typically, describes the benefits for novice teachers (Odell and Huling, 2000). However, facilitators of mentoring programmes and researchers are recognising that mentors derive substantial benefits from the mentoring experience (Resta, Huling, White and Matschek, 1997; David, 2000; Holloway, 2001). Professional development benefits the mentoring experience, which is the focus of this study. Since 1986, only a few studies have focused on the primary question of mentor benefits, but a considerable number of researchers and mentor programme evaluators have reported mentor benefits, in the realm of unanticipated or secondary, positive effects. This body of work will be briefly examined in a broader discussion of how mentoring contributes to the ongoing professional development of an experienced teacher.

The basic idea here is to talk about how mentoring as a process helps professional development. It is a slightly different concept. It is not only an induction programme, which is used generally for the induction of new/novice teachers by experienced teachers, but an ongoing process which facilitates teachers for their continuous professional development.

A teacher has to simultaneously deal with many things, including the class from different dimensions, learning new curricula, inclusion, technology, co-curricular activities and develop an association with society. These are not easy tasks and need to be persistently dealt with. These issues are not only associated with newly recruited teachers but also associated with experienced teachers. Mentoring can be used as a system to deal with such concerns.

Teachers do not share their experiences with other colleagues

Teachers' hardly perform reflective practices

Professional development programmes prevail for some particular time, which does not facilitate continuously

Teachers do not want to leave their comfort zone

Methodological improvement is not satisfactory

In-service mentoring is a process which facilitates the professional development of teachers. This professional development entails their development in knowledge, methodology, understanding children and critical understanding of their profession. Mentoring functions are carried out within the context of an ongoing, caring relationship between colleagues. It helps in producing teaching material, classroom teaching strategies and understanding teaching in a more comprehensive manner. One has to keep in mind that the ultimate aim here is to improve teaching and learning.

We have to keep in mind that when we initiate a mentoring process, there will be several issues and concerns, such as work settings, the school culture and organisation, curriculum processes, evaluation practices and so on. We have to look into the improvement of professional practices, which include effective teaching models, strategies, leadership and management skills. We have to develop the school as a learning community, having lifelong learning orientation. In this regard, we have to understand the stages of the teachers' development. It can be understood at three levels: initial orientation, improving professional practices and developing teaching, as a professional community. *Initial orientation* deals with some basic questions, such as how to plan to teach, how to organise the curriculum, managing student behaviour, etc. *Learning to improve teaching practices* involves ways to improve teaching practice, reflection in and on one's teaching. Finally, *developing a learning professional community* encourages developing an empowered learning community of learners and teachers. Teachers need to be assisted to move to the stage of *developing a learning community* passing through two earlier stages named *initial orientation* and *improved professional practices.* This is the purpose and goal of mentoring.

Mentoring is the central feature of CPD's successful progress. Without mentoring, teachers take considerable time to move to the Professional Practice and Learning Community stages. In this process, both the mentor and mentee gain from the mentoring experience. It is important to know that in this process, the hierarchical relationship between mentor and mentee needs to be unvalued. It should be clear that there will be a mutual and collegial relationship between mentor and mentee, rather than a hierarchical one. This happens in mentoring because they change their role in each other's classes and therefore collaborative spirit becomes an important factor here. Mentorship activities, structures and programmes can vary widely from mentor-mentee pairs to teams of mentors.

We need to trust that teachers have practical experience at the pedagogical level. Yet, for mentoring, they need specific kinds of skills, in order to facilitate the professional development of each other. In the mentoring process, there are particularly three types of needs: *professional needs, pedagogical needs* and *personal level needs.* Professional level needs comprise of provincial expectations, understanding about polices, roles, rights and responsibility of teachers. Pedagogical context needs to be derived from teaching, diagnosing, evaluating and maintaining, whereas personal dimension deals with the moral concerns, well-being and encouragement

The role of a mentor, therefore, becomes important. Good mentor teachers are required for an ongoing support for the school to fulfil its role. Successful mentorship depends upon the clarity of the participant's roles and responsibilities. Successful programmes have shown that mentor-mentee should:

- Develop a collaborative attitude toward each other.
- Understand the need and problems faced by colleagues.
- Have a handful of good strategies to suggest to each other in teaching.
- Discuss issues and concerns of each other's teaching, without any hesitation, in a collaborative manner.
- Develop strategies for developing themselves professionally.

Mentor and mentee have some responsibilities, too, in the process of mentoring, such as:

- They should encourage each other to feel comfortable and share their experiences freely.
- They should work in a small cluster within the school and, later, within inter-school, based on subject specific criteria.
- They should maintain a relationship with each other, according to the professional code of conduct.
- Model and demonstrate effective teaching strategies.
- Observe and provide feedback to each other before, during and after the teaching.

- Assist each other in identifying personal strengths and planning for further professional growth.
- Assist each other with curriculum and instructional planning.

Teachers are always required to be curious to know new things and should always try to implement this at work. This new learning helps them to develop their own teaching style over a period of time. To make the process successful, teachers need to develop listening and sharing skills and attitude, which help them to be committed to an ethos of collective reflective practices. They will need self-guidance, self-support, and self-analysis of their own teaching, which help them to move beyond simple day-to-day work, to a more meaningful contribution to the school and the teaching-learning process.

All responsibilities are not liable for the teachers (mentor-mentee). The school administration has a major role to play, as well. Their role will work as a key for the entire process. The school principal has the most significant role regarding administration. The principal should take the initiative to introduce a mentoring programme in school for the teachers' CPD. The principal should also inform teachers about the support they will get from the school in terms of time, resources and so on. This programme should not only be introduced to existing teachers but to newly appointed teachers as well. Along with the principal, other school administrators should contribute to the smooth functioning of this mentoring scheme. They can play an important role in evaluating the entire process.

Why Mentoring

How will it be Beneficial for Teachers	*How will it be Beneficial for Administrators*
• Access to the knowledge, experience and support for each other. • Enhanced personal and professional understanding and well-being because of a sharing attitude. • Increased self-confidence and self-esteem. • Reduction of behavioural model of trial and error for teaching and more focus on the collaborative way of teaching-learning. • A positive attitude towards teaching profession and their professional development. • Progressive and multi-dimensional outlook to the teaching-learning process. • Development of teachers as teachers instead of just different affiliation. • Development of reflective practice. • Development of self-evaluation.	• Increased performance. • Reduced the administrators' role of supervision and so on, as it will not be needed, and teachers will take care of this. • As it will be a school-based programme, there will be no need for outside agencies to intervene in the school system.

Benefits for the Profession

- It will manage to retain creative and innovative teachers.
- Retention of experienced teachers who can facilitate new teachers, in the process of CPD.
- It will develop a positive teaching ethos.
- It will help to establish the process of continuous professional development.
- Establishment of professional norms of openness to learning from others, new ideas and instructional practices, continual improvement, collaboration, collegiality and experimentation.

For Students

- It will help learners to develop learning ability.
- It helps in developing critical and reflective thinking in learners, as teachers themselves are doing this.
- As a teacher will not be authoritarian and dominating, the process will help learners to explore more and engage positively.
- Teachers will be more self-confident and aware about themselves, learner will observe teacher and can develop such ability.

How to Help Each Other

There are various dimensions of teaching in which teachers may help each other. Some of them are classroom management, pedagogical concerns, syllabus and curriculum, engagement of learners, and so on.

The mentor-mentee relationship is an equal kind of relationship, which provides equal space to both of them to develop. There are various important things one has to keep in mind, while teaching regarding classroom management, such as planning, the seating pattern in the classroom, teaching learning rules and so on. It is the responsibility of a teacher to create a positive and enthusiastic environment for learning. Overall, mentoring will help them to manage their classroom in a more effective manner. In the same way, pedagogical concerns are another important aspect of teaching. For this, resource availability, teaching planning, maintaining students' records, understanding different individual needs, and, ultimately, developing a healthy environment for learning, based on effective pedagogy which carries a thoughtful idea at the base. Syllabus and curriculum have different kinds of concerns, such as teaching content, curriculum guides, student learning and achievements. Engagement of learners is another important task that needs attention in the class, which can be done through different teaching-learning strategies (individual and cooperative). These activities should include field visits and practical aspects. All these dimensions can be taken care of effectively with the process of mentoring.

But to achieve this, we have to keep a check on ourselves. Mentoring is collaborative and should not be understood as a hierarchical relationship. It should be accepted as an ongoing process, where one level provides the basis and understanding for the next level. This process encourages self-reliance and growth, which will help teachers to evaluate and reflect upon their own practices. Mentoring should not be considered judgemental, rather it should be accepted as a very obvious process of school education for the teachers' CPD. But, it is also important to keep in mind that this relationship should respect the code of conduct developed for professional development.

Certain things are important for a mentoring programme for teachers and can be understood at various levels, such as: learning more about what is expected of one as a mentor, collecting classroom observation data, diagnosing the needs of the mentor and mentee, developing interpersonal skills that support the mentoring process, assisting each other with classroom management, helping each other to develop a variety of effective teaching strategies, using principles of adult learning to facilitate the professional growth of teachers, socialising teachers into the school culture, helping each other to maintain student discipline, helping to design a long-range plan for professional development, finding resources and materials for effective teaching, providing emotional support to each other, co-teaching, managing time and work, developing problem-solving strategies, helping to motivate students, helping each other to assist students with special needs, helping each other to deal with the needs of the learners. These points are given by Gordon (1991). How to Help Beginning Teachers to Succeed, ASCD, but have been slightly changed for the in-service mentoring programme. He had suggested these for the induction programme for newly appointed teachers.

It is important to acknowledge that the mentorship programme is intended not to supplant existing support programmes for teachers, but to enhance the system or school programmes. In this case, it will be important to identify the existing option for CPD of teachers and possibilities of improvement with new and innovative practices.

The most common concern for a mentorship programme is how to communicate support to each other without being intrusive. At the same time, mentor and mentee are concerned about burdening each other with questions. Both (mentor and mentee) need constant reassurance that they do not mind helping each other. Here are a few ideas to ease the tension:

- Complement each other.
- Take a coffee break or lunch together.
- Spend an evening together.
- Give information about ways to gain the support of key individuals.
- Give suggestions to acquire scarce resources.
- Offer an invitation for a small get-together with other colleagues.

Even after this sort of understanding with each other, a process of self-evaluation should be acknowledged by both. They may ask many questions to themselves, such as: Do you do what you say you will do? Do you show your confidence in personal or professional tasks? Do you respond to statements and questions? Do you freely talk about a topic under discussion? Do you respect the ideas of others during discussion and otherwise, even though you may not agree? Do you cross check your assumptions through paraphrasing? Do you encourage your protégé to probe for his or her own answers to be more confident? What kind of language do you use: descriptive or prescriptive? Do you provide opportunities for clarification? Are you sensitive towards different issues? Do you probe for thoughts and feelings as well as facts, while discussing professional issues? Do you encourage your partner (mentor or mentee) to be aware of more knowledge and information about the suggestions given?

Mentors and mentees need to be aware of many things, some of them are discussed here. They must believe that they can help each other, but sometimes we have to find out ways on our own. It is possible that at times, your colleague may not accept your idea. In such a situation, there is no need to feel bad. Have faith in the experiences of your colleagues. Trust the knowledge of your colleague. Do not try to prove that you know better than him/her, even if it is true. This will develop cooperation among faculty members. It is important to believe that we can help each other to become more efficient. Both (mentor and mentee) should keep an open mind for suggestions and reactions. But this should not be in the form to defaming each other. There should be an environment which make teachers realise that they need each other for their CPD. Focus should be on the progress of teachers. One should avoid patronising and judgemental remarks. Lack of time should not be the reason for being judgemental. They should get time to discuss practices. Expecting too much from teachers is inappropriate. They need clear support from the administration. The principal can help a lot in this regard.

Along with this, one should not have an ego (in popular sense) that he/she has learned because of me. These ego hassles will not favour mentoring programmes, because collective, continuous support and understanding among teachers is needed.

Pedagogical and instructional concerns are very important. Ultimately a teacher has to deal with the class and the learners. This process will make teachers reflect about their teaching of how s/he managed to constructively be engaged, so that institutional goals could be met. The teacher could think and talk about the learning and its outcomes (generally and specifically), with reference to the goals of instructional planning for a particular lesson. Questioning of one's practice and re-teaching of the same lesson with the same group with a different method. Teachers must be ready to learn from the learners too, as effective teacher would be flexible if s/he learns from his/her learners.

On the same line, certain important points need to be acknowledged regarding teachers' CPD. They should keep focus on the future and on the excitement of lifelong learning. They should think how their professional growth plan reflects their lifelong learning, how their immediate goals relate to their long-term goals. Teachers should investigate new techniques and how they can best use them in their classroom. How can they use the critical concepts to improve their teaching practice? How can they link their growth to knowledge, skills and attributes related to interim certification?

CHAPTER 15

Benefits and Challenges of Reflective Practices

Reflective practice, undoubtedly, is a process which provides an effective way for professional development and benefits practitioners and schools in several ways. These practices consist of certain problems and challenges and these mostly occur, as whenever we use any ideas in an actual situation or in actual practice, it loses its ultimate nature and we face challenges on account of the already existant scenario. The same is true with reflection and reflective practices. Considering the importance of reflection for professional development and situating it in the professional context, it becomes important to find certain solutions to the problems associated with reflective practices.

This chapter presents the benefits, challenges and possible solutions to these challenges. Bailey, Curtis, & Nunan, (1998), Crandall (2000), Farrell (1998), Stanley (1998), and Thiel (1999), among others have discussed these benefits and challenges.

Benefits of Reflective Practices

Flexibility

There are numerous differences and diversities that exist (in terms of institutional context, learner group, and curricula, resources and teacher's preparation) in our education system. Reflective practices can help deal effectively with the given diversities. It has to be organised at both individual and group levels. A good reflective practice involves the input of learners, colleagues, and others, because of its collective nature and is important for both the novice and experienced teachers. Novice teachers can know and evaluate their achievement and experienced teachers can work upon self-awareness and development for CPD.

Practicality

Reflective practices do not provide an immediate solution in the beginning, but, once a person has engaged in the process of reflection, an immediate solution can be located, and a healthy relationship can be developed between teaching and CPD. This happens because reflective practices require a person to see and visualise the relationship or connection between the current context with its benefits and also what can be done to make it better and viable in terms of efficiency. It is important to mention here that experimentation with new techniques, ideas, and approaches are fundamental of the process, where developing a link between theories and practice are crucial. This relationship provides opportunities to deal with issues and concerns regarding CPD. It is suggested that the practitioners share their own insight and personal theories of teaching.

Professionalism

Continuous interaction of intellect, responsibility and professionalism are the key aspects of reflective practices. It continuously tries to establish a connection with theory, to enhance practice. These theories help to develop and use tools, to analyse the existing situations for progressive change in one's personal as well as professional life. These theories provide opportunities to react to their own teaching processes during execution. This kind of engagement provides space and opportunities to learn more skills and develop more enhanced abilities to CPD.

Sustainability

There is a need for the sustainable development of teachers, rather than discrete workshops and conferences. This sustenance will only be achieved, if we work towards enabling teachers themselves with skills, such as 'Reflective Practice', which creates a cyclical process that allows time for reflection, implementation, and follow-up. It centres on development, skills and attitudes that eventually become a regular part of good teaching. Once mastered, it should be integrated with regular teaching responsibilities, resulting in even better satisfaction and efficiency.

Support of Scientific Methodology Oriented Views

If you have support of sound methodological practice (based on the scientific method), you might expect reflective practice to have empirical data to support it; you might want to test the hypotheses of research studies which investigates its effectiveness, or look at some statistical data from being an interesting theory, to a scientifically useful, investigative tool. Personal change and effectiveness are not something easily measurable in statistical terms – there is though a wealth of evidence on the effectiveness of reflective practice, based on the views of individual practitioners, which may help you assess how you could use reflective practice.

Challenges and Possible Solutions

Lack of Time and Space to Reflect

Lack of time and space is an ever-present problem in education for practitioners, at all stages of the implementation of any strategy. Making time for reflective practice is not easy, but it is essential to offer the best service to learners and improve your own career path. Some common solutions are:

- using the journey to and from your workplace to reflect,
- using the first 20 minutes, after your learners have left for the day, while events are still fresh in your mind,
- jotting down notes in a journal to reflect on, when you have time, later in the week,
- talking with a trusted and honest colleague over lunch or a group discussion with several colleagues at the beginning or end of the week.

Negative Preconceptions

It is common to find negative preconceptions about reflective practice. This is because it can be a difficult and time-consuming process and it may take a long time to show real results. If you have negative preconceptions, discuss them with colleagues, who use reflective practice, and see whether their experiences change your opinion.

Also, consider trying it for yourself, over a period of time, such as a term, and see whether you can identify changes to your own practice.

Fear

Reflective practice can be an intimidating idea, as it requires a critical, honest and open view of yourself, which can be difficult. Many forms of reflective practice are entirely private; your colleagues will not see it or judge you on the basis of it. If you find it difficult to be honest with yourself, see whether you can find a trusted and honest colleague, who can become your 'critical friend' and help you identify situations or skills, which could be improved.

Risk of it becoming a routine, without any real thought

Reflective practice should never be done as a simple 'tick box' activity. Real change comes from hard work and determination to improve. It would be better for you to reflect less and do it right, then go through the motions every day, without thinking about it.

Lack of knowledge and experience, regarding how to reflect

This can be a problem for both new and experienced practitioners, alike. Although reflective practice is taught for most professional teaching qualifications, you need practice to be able to do it well. You could brush up on some of the theories discussed and use some of the techniques to practise with. Certain reflective techniques suit some people more than others – see what works for you.

Seeing it as a 'success or failure' approach

You should not see the work you do with learners, as either a success or a failure. With reflective practice, you can begin to see that, even if things did not go so well, you have ample opportunity to improve over the course of your career. If you start to take the reflective view that every situation, no matter how painful, can be learned from, you will have the right mindset to improve.

Worry of becoming introspective and anxious about your practice

Reflective practice is a critical process and looking for an area to develop and improve upon, can be unsettling. If you approach it with the mindset of actively wanting to improve, rather than dwelling on what did not go so well, you should not have a problem with being anxious. Here the role of support structures, such as positive support of an institute where one works, are crucial to put one out of such a self-doubting state, which is bound to happen, if we seriously follow reflective process.

Organisational Culture

Some educational establishments are supportive of reflective practice and their seniors will model reflective behaviour themselves in improving their organisation. Other educational establishments do not value this approach. At the level of the individual practitioner, however, the aim of reflective practice is not about changing the culture of your organisation, but about changing your own practice and skills. Do not be put off by a culture, which does not embrace this.

A very effective and yet not too demanding way to ensure benefits of reflective practice, is PLC. (Professional Learning Community)

Professional Learning Community (PLC)

PLC refers to a model where school capacities are seen and grounded in the culture of the school and staff of the school. This model is based on the cooperative learning design, given by Peter Senge (1990), which talks about the teacher's workplace culture. These authors postulated that when all the personnel of a work unit are involved in setting the vision and determining what the staff needs to do to accomplish the vision, there would be continuous learning of the staff and thereby continuous benefits to clients and constituents. It distributes responsibility to the group, based on collective learning. It carries the essential function of providing support structure for reflective practitioners (emotional, motivational, infrastructure and so on).

Creating a professional learning community in a school is no easy task. There must be some basic elements which guarantee the success of any PLC, such as:

Trust: It is certainly important to have faith and trust on peer colleagues. The level of faith should be such that one can share all concerns freely. This should be reflected in a shared mission, vision, values and goals.

Collaborative Culture: Professionals, in a learning community, work in teams that share a common purpose. They learn from each other and create the momentum that drives improvement. Such collaboration is necessary among students and teachers, between academics and administrative staff, between school and personnel outside the school and between the school and community. This process is essentially based on mutual honest communication, sharing knowledge and deep association and concern with the school. A deliberate effort to develop trust will develop a better professional learning community.

Teachers should be heard: The school, where the teachers' voices are heard, is an agency to practise their understanding and knowledge, and should not only promote, but maintain the process of collective learning. If the administration in school does not consult with teachers, it will be an autocratic leadership. Consultation with teachers will facilitate the process positively. PLC can become successful in such a collaborative environment. In brief, we can say that the success of PLC is associated with the teachers' views, perspectives and commitment. A truly successful PLC would start from the teachers' level, their views, their perspectives towards maximising students' learning.

Student Centred: There is no doubt that the idea of child centred education, where the child agency is respected, is good. The democratic function of a school, with reference to students, will develop a better learning community. Many issues, related to administrative and academics, can be resolved by accepting the learners' space in school. Such spaces will help in developing confident learners, who respect knowledge and collaborative action. The fundamental question is, "Is it better for children?" PLC will tend to the particular needs and culture of their school with an easy and natural take on benefits and could more easily integrate theory and understanding to practice.

Action Oriented/Experimentation: Members of professional learning communities, constantly, turn their learning and insights into action. They should recognise the importance of engagement and experience in learning and in testing new ideas. It tunes our practices towards a continuous growth of our profession.

It should not be just any other 'Add On' Programme: This process should not be simply an addition to already existing programmes. It should not overburden teachers. A change is required to the existing system, to develop spaces for collaborative action. The school and school authorities should be cooperative in this process, rather than resisting it. This support will surely prove beneficial for learners, teachers and the school, as a whole.

Commitment to Continuous Improvement: Members of a learning organisation are not content with the status quo and continually seek ways to bring the present reality closer to the future ideal. They constantly ask themselves and each other:

- What is our purpose?
- What do we hope to achieve?
- What are our strategies for improving?
- How will we assess our efforts?

In a professional learning community, educators create an environment that fosters mutual cooperation, emotional support, and personal growth, as they work together to achieve what they cannot accomplish alone.

All programmes, associated with continuous professional development, have some strengths and weaknesses. It is important to see these critically, in order that a better CPD, based on reflective processes, can be established, where no one is forced to become a part of it, instead, they can choose to become a part of it for their continuous professional development.

References

Andrew, M. D. (1997). What Matters Most for Teacher Educators? *Journal of Teacher Education*, 48, 167-176.

Barton, D. & Tusting, K. (2005). *Beyond Communities of Practice: Language, Power and Social Context.* New York: CUP.

Beaty, L. (1997). *Developing Your Teaching Through Reflective Practice.* Birmingham: SEDA.

Bentley, T. (1995). *Facilitation: Providing Opportunities for Learning.* London: McGraw-Hill.

Biggs, J. & Tang, C. (2007). *Teaching for Quality Learning.* Berkshire: SRHE & Open University Press.

Biglan, A. (1973a). The Characteristics of Subject Matter in Different Scientific Areas, *Journal of Applied Psychology*, 57, 195-203

Boyd, E. & Fales, A. (1983). Learning: The key to Learning from Experience. *Journal of Humanistic Psychology*, 23(2), 99-117

Britt, M.S., Irwin, K.C., Ritchie, G. (2001). Professional Conversations and Professional Growth. *Journal of Mathematics Teacher Education Netherlands* 4: 29-53 (study 351).

Brookfield, S. D. (1987). *Developing Critical Thinkers: Challenging Adults to Explore Alternative Ways of Thinking and Acting.* Milton Keynes: Open University Press.

Bruner, J. S. (1966). *Toward a Theory of Instruction.* Cambridge, MA: Harvard University Press.

Carr, D. (2000). *Professionalism and Ethics in Teaching.* London: Routledge.

Carr, W. (1995). *For Education: Towards Critical Educational Inquiry.* London: Falmer

Darling-Hammond, L. (1993) Reframing the School Reform Agenda: Developing Capacity for School Transformation. *Phi Delta Kappan*, 74, 752-761.

Dewey, J. (1902). *The School and Society.* Chicago: University of Chicago Press.

Dhankar, R. (2013). Teacher Plus; *The Magazine for Contemporary Teacher.* New Delhi

Elliott, J. (1991). *Action Research for Educational Change.* Milton Keynes: Open University Press.

Ertmer, P.A., Hruskocy, C. (1999). Impacts of a University-elementary School Partnership Designed to Support Technology Integration. *Educational Technology Research and Development* 47: 81-96 (study 357).

Freire, P. (1971). *Pedagogy of the Oppressed.* New York: Continuum.

Fullan, M. (1991). *The New Meaning of Educational Change.* London: Cassell.

Fullan, M.G. (1990). Staff Development, Innovation, and Institutional Development. In B. Joyce (Ed.), *Changing school culture through staff development* (1990) Yearbook of the Association for Supervision and Curriculum Development, pp. 3-25). Alexandria, VA: ASCD.

Fullan, M.G. (1993). *Change Forces: Probing the Depths of Educational Reform.* London, U.K.: Falmer Press.

Gersten, R., Morvant, M., Brengelman, S. (1995). Close to the Classroom is Close to the bone: Coaching as A Means to Translate Research into Classroom Practice. *Exceptional Children* 62: 52-66 (study 359).

Gibbs, G. (1998). *Learning by Doing: A Guide of Teaching and Learning Methods.* Oxford: Oxford University Press.

Goodson, I. F., & Hargreaves, A. (1996). *Teachers' Professional Lives.* London: The Falmer Press.

Guskey, T., Huberman, M. (1995). *Professional Development in Education.* London: Teachers College Press.

Habermas, J. (1971). *Knowledge and Human Interests.* Boston: Beacon Press.

Harvey, S. (1999) The Impact of Coaching in South African Primary Science INSET. *International Journal of Educational Development* 19: 191-205 (study 360).

Hatton, N. & Smith, D. (1995) Reflection in Teacher Education-towards Definition and Implementation. *Teaching and Teacher Education,* 11, (1) 33-49.

Heichel, L. G., and Miller, T.M. (1993). The Importance of Reflection in Decision-making. In *Teachers are Researchers: Reflection and Action,* (ed.), L. Patterson, C. M. Santa, K. G. Short, and K. Smith, 173-82. Newar.

Henry, G. (1988). *Teachers as Transformatory Intellectuals.* London: Bergin and Garvey.

Hoban, G. (2000). Making Practice Problematic: Listening to Student Interviews as a Catalyst for Teacher Reflection. *Journal of Teacher Education* 28: 133-147.

Johns, C. (2000) *Becoming a Reflective Practitioner.* Oxford: Blackwell Science.

Kolb, D. (1984). *Experiential Learning.* New Jersey: Prentice Hall.

Kolb, D (1984). *Experiential Learning as the Science of Learning and Development.* New Jersey: Prentice Hall.

Kolb, D. A. (1984). *Experiential Learning.* Englewood Cliffs: NJ Prentice-Hall.

Kolb, D. A. (1984). *Experiential learning: Experience as the Source of Learning and Development.* Englewood Cliffs, NJ: Prentice-Hall.

Kreber, C. (2005). Reflection on Teaching and the Scholarship of Teaching: Focus on Science Instructors. *Higher Education,* 50 (2), 323-359. doi: 10. 1007/s 10734-004-6360-2.

Krol, A. Christine (1997). Coming to Terms: Reflective Practice. *The English Journal,* 86 (5), 96-97.

Kumar, S. (2015). *Child Development and Pedagogy.* New Delhi: Pearson.

Little, J.W. (1982). Norms of Collegiality and Experimentation: Workplace Conditions of School Success. *American Educational Research Journal,* 19, 325-340.

Little, J.W. (1993). Teachers' Professional Development in a Climate of Educational Reform. *Educational Evaluation and Policy Analysis,* 15, 129-151.

Louis, K.S., & Miles, M.B. (1990). *Improving the Urban High School: What Works and Why.* New York: Teachers College Press.

Maughan, C., & Webb, J. (2001). *Small Group Learning and Assessment.* Retrieved on August 01, 2007, from the Higher Education Academy, Web site: http://www.ukcle.ac.uk/resources/temp/assessment.html

McAlpine, L., Weston, C., Berthiaume, D., Fairbank-Roch, G., & Owen, M. (2004). *Reflection on Teaching: Types and Goals of Reflection. Educational Research and Evaluation,* 70(4), 337-363. doi: 10.1080/13803610512331383489.

Miller, L., & Silvemail, D.L. (1994). Wells Junior High School: Evolution of a professional development school. In L. Darling-Hammond (Ed.), *Professional Development Schools: Schools for Developing a Profession* (pp. 28-49). New York: Teachers College Press.

Moon, J. A. (2000). *Reflection in Learning and Professional Development.* London, UK: Kogan Page.

NCF (2005). *National Curriculum Framework.* Delhi: National Council for Educational Research and Training.

NCFTE (2005). *National Curriculum Framework for Teacher Education.* Delhi: National Council for Teacher Education.

Pollard, A. (2005). *Reflective Teaching.* London: Continuum.

Rod, B. & Amol, P. (2013). *Continuing Professional Development: Lessons from India (Ed.)* New Delhi: British Council.

Rodgers, C. (2002). *Defining Reflection: Another Look at John Dewey and Reflective Thinking.* New York.

Schön, D. A. (1983). *The Reflective Practitioner: How Professionals Think in Action.* New York: Basic Books.

Schön, D. A. (1987). *Educating the Reflective Practitioner.* San Francisco, CA: Jossey-Bass.

Slavin, R.E., Madden, N.A., Dolan, L.J. (1996). *Every Child, Every School, Success for All.* Thousand Oaks, CA, California: Corwin Press.

Sparks, D., & Loucks-Horsley, S. (1989). Five models of staff development for teachers. *Journal of Staff Development,* 10(4), 40-57.

Stenhouse, L. (1967). *Culture and Education.* London: Nelson.

Stephens, D., & K. M. Reimer. (1993). Explorations in Reflective Practice. In *Teachers are Researchers: Reflection and action, ed. L. Patterson.* 160-72. Newark, DE: International Reading Association.

Vygotsky, L.S. (1980). *Mind in Society: The Development of Higher Psychological Processes.* Cambridge, Mass., USA: Harvard University Press.

Index